WHY WORK ISN'T WORKING ANYMORE

Three Tools To Transform Your Workplace As If People Mattered

WHY WORK ISN'T WORKING ANYMORE

*Three Tools To Transform Your Workplace
As If People Mattered*

By

Jim Karger and Fritz Aldrine

ISBN: 1-58961-258-2

Published by PageFree Publishing, Inc.
109 South Farmer Street
Otsego, MI 49078
(269) 692-3926
www.pagefreepublishing.com

"We come into this world as the result of others' actions. We survive here in dependence on others. Whether we like it or not, there is hardly a moment of our lives when we do not benefit from others' activities. For this reason, it is hardly surprising that most of our happiness arises in the context of our relationships with others. Nor is it so remarkable that our greatest joy should come when we are motivated by concern for others... In our concern for others, we worry less about ourselves. When we worry less about ourselves, the experience of our own suffering is less intense."

His Holiness, The Dalai Lama,
"Ethics For A New Millennium"

This book is for managers committed to making the workplace a better place.

CONTENTS

PART I - WHY WORK ISN'T WORKING ANYMORE

Why do more than half of all employees find little satisfaction in their work? Why has the number of employees who are "reasonably satisfied" with their jobs plunged dramatically in the last decade? What about you? How much satisfaction do you find in your work and your job?

Why is work not an "end" for most employees, but just a "means" to another end? Why is work just a way to "make a living" for most employees? Why are we given so many reasons why we should be satisfied with work, and why aren't those reasons working?

PART II - MYTHS OF WORK

Is work "meaningful"? Is your work "meaningful"? Are you one of the handful of *Givers, Creators,* and *Builders* whose work provides "inner meaning"? Or do you drag yourself to work each day for a reason other than a soul-fed love for what you do? Would you do the job you are doing today if there was no paycheck? If not, why don't you do something else?

Do you work because there's nothing better to do? Do you believe evil lurks to snare those who have too much time on their hands? Without work, would terminal boredom set in? Would you die with your face in the soup, having fallen asleep on life if you stopped working tomorrow? Could you fill up all the hours in a day without your job? If so, what would you do?

Do you believe that quantity of stuff equals quality of life, that if you owned more you'd be happier, that if you lived in a bigger house you'd be more satisfied, and that if you won the lottery there would be a permanent smile on your face? Are you like many employees who dislike their jobs, despise their bosses, and find work to be a mundane drudgery, but work for the paycheck? Do you believe that paycheck is going to bring you satisfaction tomorrow that you don't feel today? Do you work so one day you won't have to work any more? Instead of asking yourself just where the work-and-spend cycle is going to lead, are you speeding up, running ever faster, chasing the dream that "more" will one day become "enough"? Will employers garner the guts to step up and open themselves to the possibility that their focus should not be making humans better "resources," but help to become better, happier human beings?

PART III - "REAL LIFE," "WORK LIFE," ALL OF LIFE: WHAT SATISFIES US?

Is there a functional alternative to the "work-and-spend cycle" that is making few happy? What human dynamic provides you the most satisfaction in your life? If you didn't work, would you spend more time with your family and friends? Would you get to know your neighbors? Would you enjoy spending more time with those for whom you care the most? Is there a common thread in our lives that leads to satisfaction? If so, what is that thread and why is it absent in most workplaces?

Why does corporate America continue to pander to the *Myth of More,* playing the "cash card," leading employees to believe that "more" money and benefits are right around the corner, even though there hasn't been "more" for a long, long time? Why do most employers continue playing the shell game, trying to make less look like more? Why have personal connections between managers and employees been sublimated, even discouraged, when that connection is most predictive of employee satisfaction?

If most managers know relationships are important, even essential to workplace satisfaction, why do they know more about characters on TV than they know about their own employees? Why do managers plead "no time" or regurgitate the age-old adage that "we shouldn't get too close to our employees" to justify not knowing them? Why do these excuses fail when put under the microscope?

PART IV - THE RELATIONSHIP-BASED MANAGER'S TOOLBOX

Is there a way managers can enjoy positive, purposeful relationships with each of their employees? What part does knowing and remembering significant events in the lives of others play in relationship development? Is there a simple way for managers to record milestone events in the lives of their employees? Is there a way to easily recall these events? Once recalled, how should a manager utilize the information in the creation of meaningful workplace relationships?

What do we know about those with whom we enjoy the best relationships – their challenges, our common interests? What do we commonly do for those with whom we enjoy the best relationships – empathize, lend an ear, help in personal and professional development? Can managers recall important information about each of their employees and from it understand employee actions and reactions, evaluate employee conduct when it doesn't make sense, motivate employees with their own anecdotes, and find and address endemic problems in the workplace? Can managers learn empathy—to see what their employees see, to feel what they feel, and naturally nurture meaningful relationships?

Is there a palpable way for managers to express care, compassion, and concern? Is there a need for something beyond speech? Are speaking and writing different qualitatively? Unlike speaking, does writing compel us to refine our thoughts, feelings and opinions before expressing them? What is the impact of recognizing in writing the most important events in the lives of employees and their families? What are the hurdles to penning personal correspondence to employees? Can the hurdles be leapt? What is the impact of writing on the relationship between managers and employees?

Are the *Milestone Box, Manager's Journal,* and *Care Cards* independent tools of purposeful relationships, or are they synergistic, each magnifying the others' effectiveness? How can companies effectively roll out, train, and implement the tools in their workplaces? Should the tools be implemented one at a time or simultaneously? How can managers maximize the effectiveness of the tools—individually and working together? How should managers explain the tools to their employees?

PART V - CONCLUSION
WHERE DO WE GO FROM HERE?

Where does relationship-based management lead? What does it accomplish? Can kindness be its own motive? Can we change the way we believe by changing the way we act? Can managing and caring coexist in today's competitive workplace? Can we find meaning in our work through meaningful relationships? Where does the relationship-based manager fit into the future of the American workplace?

ACKNOWLEDGEMENTS

From Jim:

Thanks to Kelly for the title, and her support, compassion, and insight throughout this project; Kim Harrison, my loyal assistant for many years; Bob Deitz for his assistance in developing an early outline; Bernie Koehne and Jake Nolin for their early reviews of the manuscript; Michael Cohen for the refocus; Richard Kirschner and Jim Lavish for rolling out the program before it was a proven commodity; Andy Lang for his guidance on understanding the American employee; Hank Biedenharn for giving a 24-year-old kid-lawyer a chance a long time ago; Spencer Robinson for being my best friend; Bob Furge for helping me understand that everything is as it should be; and my colleague, Fritz, who reminds me of the importance of spontaneity and humor in living a good life.

From Fritz:

Thanks to my wife, Stacey, my family, and my friends for joining me in a happy life; to Ronald King, Sam Lindsay, and Mark Southerst for proving that compassion, happiness, and professionalism can coexist in the workplace; and to Jim for showing me a new way of thinking—about everything.

And, lest we forget the most important people involved in this project, we thank all the managers with whom we have been privileged to work and from whom we have learned more than we have taught. You know who you are.

-Jim Karger and Fritz Aldrine

INTRODUCTION

LESS than half of all employees today are satisfied with their jobs. After years of meager raises, cuts in benefits, and mass layoffs, it should not be surprising that most employees do not believe their employers care about them beyond their utility as "human resources."

Most companies have done nothing about the precipitous decline in employee morale. Most deny it exists, at least within their own organizations. Others sit back and hope the problem will resolve itself. Still others have tried to reverse the spiral with fancy mission statements, renominating employees as "team-members," making "less" look like "more," and balancing "work" and "life," as if those were two different experiences. None of the institutional solutions implemented by corporate America have been effective, leaving most companies whistling past the graveyard, painting a smiley face on the problem of employee unhappiness and hoping something will change, but not knowing what that something may be.

That is what this book is about: why work isn't working anymore for most employees, how companies have failed to reverse the decline in employee satisfaction by playing their weakest hand, and how you can make a difference—not by covering up the problem, denying it, or justifying it—but by empowering yourself and your managers to effect positive change in the lives of others.

In Part I we examine why work isn't working anymore—why a majority of employees are not satisfied with their work experience. In Part II, we scrutinize the myths of work that bring employees to work but haven't made them happy there. In Part III, we look at a simple but powerful human dynamic that is inextricably linked to life satisfaction, and we examine how and why it is missing in most workplaces. In Part IV, we provide three simple tools to managers that will bring this dynamic into play within the workplace. Finally, in Part V, we conclude with expectations and a meditation on what the workplace can become if we will but focus on that which matters: each other.

The tools we introduce—*Milestone Box*, *Manager's Journal*, and *Care Cards*—have been used effectively by thousands of managers, but it has only been in the last few years that we have discovered their interdependencies and synergistic capabilities and created a comprehensive system of relationship-based management around them.

As you begin a journey that has led other managers and their employees to a more compassionate, more rewarding work experience, we ask one thing—that you remain open. Some of what you read may not come as good news. You may find some of our criticisms too harsh. You may have learned the art of management differently. You may feel angry. You may feel sad. You may object to any new initiative or requirement that mandates that you spend another minute at work. That's OK. Just give us a fair, uninterrupted read, remembering that if we continue to do things in the same old ways we can expect nothing more than the same old results—the continued slide into the abyss of workplace discontent. In order to achieve a different end, we all must be open to a different way.

Jim Karger
San Miguel de Allende, Guanajuato, Mexico
June, 2004

PART I

Why Work
Isn't Working Anymore

CHAPTER 1

Work: That Giant Sucking Sound

Work? It sucks! Why? Let's start with cubicles—those padded cells without doors, poor communications, backstabbing, unclear work expectations, inconsistent policies, changes without explanation, upper management incompetence, poorly communicated policies, the attitude of "divide and conquer" that makes employees distrust management and each other, political correctness, invasion of privacy, excessive workloads, office politics, commuting, meetings, bureaucracy, rules that make no sense, discrimination, lack of recognition, and the boredom that comes from work that requires no creativity. Frankly, all that might be livable but for the fact that no one here gives a damn about me!

- Paul, 1ˢᵗ Line Supervisor, Night Shift, Foundry

"WORK sucks!"

We've all heard that before. Most of us have said it. Today, more than half of all employees in the United States do not find their jobs even "reasonably satisfying."[i] So, if you didn't get up this morning rearing to get to work, it may be sad, but it is normal.

Happiness, satisfaction, and contentment with work have been falling for years. The Conference Board, a highly regarded business research organization, regularly surveys Americans on how satisfied they are with their lives, including their work lives. In 1995 their survey indicated that 59 percent of workers were "reasonably satisfied" with their jobs. Not ecstatic, not happy, not content, but "reasonably satisfied."

By 2000, the number of employees "reasonably satisfied" with their jobs plunged to 51 percent. In 2003 the number fell to less than half, the lowest percentage of satisfied employees since the Conference Board began its survey.[ii] Even among workers who enjoy the largest paychecks, contentment with work fell more than 10 percent in less than a decade.[iii]

So unsatisfying is work for most employees today that fully half say they would choose a lower-paying job they like over a higher-paying job they hate,[iv] yet few make that leap. Why? Because most employees have far too much stuff they have bought but not paid for. Others want more stuff. Others are simply trying to survive. Regardless of reason, most employees start each morning the same way—hit the "snooze" button on the alarm clock at least three times, get up, trudge to the job, find little or no satisfaction or happiness there, smile when the boss is looking, grit their teeth when he's not, collect their paycheck on Friday, and repeat the cycle until retirement, burn out, or death— whichever comes first.

What about you? How much do you *like* your work and your job? What about your co-workers? What about your employees?

Before answering these questions, understand that we are not asking how much you *need* your job. We're not asking whether your job *pays* enough, or whether your 401(k) gives you a warm and fuzzy feeling that one day it will provide you a ticket out of the work-a-day world.

We are asking, "How much do you *like* your job?"

"Compared to what?" one manager retorted. It is a fair question. So, let's put it another way. If you had a choice today, would you:

- Get up to an alarm in the morning and go to work, or would you sleep in?
- Work by the hour, selling your life off in eight hour increments, or spend that time with the ones you love?
- Punch a clock, run a machine, clean toilets, program a computer, listen to customers complain endlessly, or discover your vocational passion and pursue it?
- Bicker and haggle over details of business or consider the bigger picture, what it means, and how you fit in?
- Spend the rest of your life trying to make the rich richer or help those who were dealt a poor hand of cards?
- Live (and perhaps die) under artificial light in a cube farm or spend your time outside in the fresh air?
- Travel the never-ending commute to a place you despise or walk to somewhere you really want to be?
- Chase airplanes, stare at maps in rental cars, and wake up in hotels far away from home, or live life like it was not a race?
- Bite your lip when someone up the ladder takes credit for your work, or set about doing meaningful things in your life where who gets credit doesn't matter?
- Suffer in a world of "divide and conquer" where cut-throat competition is standard operating procedure, or create a world where peace, not conflict, is the norm?
- Fear being laid off, or live a simpler life, one in which you don't have to work everyday in order to just pay the bills?

In light of your answers, just how much do you like your work and your job?

If you would not show up at work tomorrow, given these alternatives, you are not alone. How many people do you know who are passionate about their work, feel appreciated, secure, cared for as a person, so much so that they want to work for their company and their boss for another ten years? Write that number down. Now, how many people do you know who suffer anxiety, resentment, anger, even depression from the stresses and pressures of their jobs, people who would quit their jobs today if they could still meet their financial responsibilities tomorrow?[v] Compare the two numbers.

We rest our case. Work isn't working for most people today.

Why? It is a question we ask everyday, and this is what we hear:

- "I decided what I was going to do when I was young, before I really knew what work was all about."
- "I never discovered my passion in life. I went to work instead."
- "I know what I'd like to do, but I don't think I could make a living doing it."
- "I liked my job in the beginning, but over the years I've gotten tired of it."
- "My work has changed."
- "My boss has changed."
- "I've changed. What was important to me at 21 isn't what is important to me at 50."
- "I'm good at what I do. I don't know how to do anything else."

Or, perhaps like millions of others in the workplace you don't get much satisfaction from your job because like most jobs, your job was designed to maximize efficiency and productivity, not to satisfy you or make you happy.

There are a plethora of reasons as to why work isn't working anymore, and after years of working with thousands of managers, we know there is is a simple, human dynamic, that when introduced systematically into the workplace will make work better for everyone. But before we look for answers to the problems of work, let's begin at the beginning and ask, "Why isn't work more than a paycheck for most employees today?"

CHAPTER 2

Work: Why It's Not More Than A Paycheck After All

I tell my kids each night before bed, "Don't work for money. Don't sell out!" I took my job because it paid better than most. Soon I was hooked on the cash, just as sure as if it were heroin. Society told me, "Go ahead and buy a new car or house—or both! You don't need the money right now. We'll lend you the dough for all of it. Just sign here. I did, and now I'm 55, have a few thousand dollars in savings, my 401(k) is in the tank, and I look at what I do for a living and know I've wasted a life—mine.

Don, Production Manager,
Automotive Parts

LIKE Don, work is not an *end* for most of us. We don't work for the sake of working. We don't work because we love what we are doing. Rather, we work as a *means* to an end, something we do in order to obtain something else.

What "something else" is that?

The American Dream, of course—being "well off" financially.[vi] Indeed, "success" in America is so often measured in economic terms that the measuring stick is rarely questioned, with more people than ever defining "the good life" as having more money and the stuff more money will buy.[vii] Between 1967 and 1990, Americans entering college who said it was essential to be "very well off financially" rose from 44 percent to 74 percent. Those who believed it was essential to develop "a meaningful philosophy of life" dropped from 83 percent to 43 percent.

It is not surprising. From childhood forward we have been relentlessly programmed to want more stuff—and we when get the stuff we want, we have learned never to be satisfied with it, but to want more and different stuff, be it a hot meal or a new Cadillac. We must have money to buy more stuff, and that is where work comes into the picture. We get jobs and work to earn the money for the current crop of stuff we want.

"Stuff?" What stuff? Well, everyone's stuff is different and the stuff we're told by manufacturers and service providers we should want depends on where each of us is on the economic ladder. For example, if you are paid minimum wage, your "stuff" may be food, a small apartment, and some used clothing from the Goodwill store. If you make a million dollars a year, your stuff may be a weekend house in the Hamptons and a second Mercedes-Benz. If you are somewhere in between, your stuff is in between, too, and the kind of work you do determines what kind of stuff you have and want. In the broadest perspective, there are two classifications of workers who use work to meet their needs (and wants) for stuff: *Survivors* and *Achievers.*

Survivors—"Just Food, Shelter, and Clothing, Please."

If you are one of the 42 million workers in the United States who lives from paycheck to paycheck, you don't have much stuff. You are a "Survivor." You work because you know that if you miss your next paycheck, what meager stuff you do have will start disappearing: car repossessed, eviction notice, writs jammed under your door, bank account seized. Your life is lived hand-to-mouth in fear.

You most likely belong to a non-exclusive club called "the working poor." According to the Economic Policy Institute, if you earn less than $16.11 an hour as a two-parent, two-child family in the United States, you are working full-time but find it difficult to maintain a safe and decent standard of living.[viii] Nearly 30 percent of all American families with children younger than age 12 with one or more parents are working to keep their heads above water and not drown in their own debt.[ix]

Work to a Survivor is a means to an end—the end of not being hungry or homeless. A Survivor doesn't worry about buying a new car; he worries about keeping his car running or paying for next month's bus pass. Survivors don't complain about low-quality health insurance or moan about the limited formulary of their prescription drug plan. Primary medical care for millions of Survivors is found in the emergency rooms of local hospitals.

The good news is that many Survivors eventually pull themselves up by their bootstraps, usually with some help, so they are no longer just surviving. They move into the other category of workers—*Achievers*—the economic fork in the road where *needs* are met and w*ants* become the primary focus, those for whom the operative, imperative verb form "to want" describes the most significant dynamic in their lives, and where the question is asked, "Why am I not happy at work?"

Achievers—"On the Ladder of Success, Always Looking Up"

If you bought this book, odds are you are not a Survivor. Rather, you are one of the vocal majority for whom work means *more* than a roof over your head and food on your table—something beyond being holed up in the dead letter office in a basement mailroom, flipping burgers, or watching a machine for a few bucks an hour.

As an *Achiever,* you are ambitious, driven by success, and relentlessly materialistic. You define yourself by what you have and what you want to have. You use "need" and "want" interchangeably. The line drawn between "needs" and "wants" has become so blurred by Achievers that more than a quarter of workers earning more than $100,000 a year say they cannot afford to buy everything they actually "need." Theirs is not the "need" of putting shoes on their children, but the "need" to put Nike shoes on their children. Achievers do not understand "need" in a literal sense, i.e., food, shelter, and clothing, but only by way of comparison to others, usually others who have more stuff than they do.

Achievers usually judge their success by using a simple equation: do I have more this year than I did this time last year? Because the answer should be "yes," Achievers work harder, make more, and buy more stuff, and on one count, they should be congratulated. Achievers are responsible for the unprecedented growth of the economy which depends on them making more money year after year, and spending it. Unfortunately, their productive efforts and the money they earn in excess of what they literally, not comparatively, "need" have not resulted in an equal amount of joy or satisfaction in their work lives. Indeed, "even as the gross domestic product [has] more than doubled in the past 30 years, the proportion of the population describing itself as 'very happy' declined by about 5 percent, or some 14 million people," [x]

How can that be? We Achievers *should* be happy at work. We are the fortunate ones, after all. We're not struggling to put food on the table. We have meaningful work to accomplish. We have work that keeps us from getting bored. We have jobs that will one day pay enough so we will finally have the "stuff" we really want.

Right?

Wrong. If where you were on the economic ladder was determinative of your satisfaction and happiness, you would find the happiest people in the world living in the biggest houses and driving the fanciest cars, and as we will discuss in Chapter 5, that is not the case. The *Myth of More* is endemic, just as the *Myth of Meaningful Work,* and the *Myth of Too Much Time*—all reasons we're told we should be satisfied with our work, reasons we should be happy on the job, but aren't.

PART II

Myths Of Work

CHAPTER 3

The Myth Of Meaningful Work

"Our high school guidance counselor used to ask us what we'd do if we had a million dollars and didn't have to work. And invariably whatever you'd say, that was supposed to be your career. So, if you wanted to fix old cars, you were supposed to be an auto mechanic."

"So, what did you say?"

"I never had an answer. I guess that's why I'm working at Inotech."

"No, you're working at Inotech because that question is bullshit to begin with. If everyone listened to her, there would be no janitors, because no one would clean up shit if they had a million dollars."

"Office Space," directed by Mike Judge[vi]

"NO one would clean toilets if they had a million dollars." That is not a myth. That is as close as it gets to universal vocational truth. Yet a lot of people do clean toilets for a living, along with thousands of other tasks and jobs that no one would perform if they had a million dollars.

How about you? Do you clean toilets for a living? No? What do you do for a living, and how is your job different than cleaning toilets? If you go to work for a paycheck, if your time and toil is just a trade for money, perhaps there is little or no qualitative difference between your work and the work of the guy who cleans toilets.

You may disagree. Most do, asserting "My job is different. My job is 'meaningful!'" Or, "My job is 'important!'"

Let's examine those claims. Is your job more "important" than cleaning toilets? If so, why is it more important? Is it more important because someone will pay you more money? Surely, that can't be the standard of an "important" job. Otherwise, we'd have to agree that the guy who takes way too many steroids and hits a ball with a stick for a living has a more important job than the President of the United States, or any world leader, for that matter.

Or perhaps you believe your job is more important because it requires greater skills than the custodian's job. That may be the case, but so what? Your skills are not so valuable or unique that you cannot be replaced, are they? Oh, it may take a week or two longer to replace you than to replace the custodian, but you can be replaced and you know it. If your job is more important than cleaning toilets, it is only more important by a few hours or a few days— the length of time it would take to find someone else to do the job you are doing now.

Let's face it. If you were run over by a bus tonight, other than the impact on your family and friends, would your company and co-workers suffer long because you didn't show up for work tomorrow? Or would you be another example of Frank Skinner's observation on self-importance that "at the end of the day, the size of the crowd at your funeral will be largely dictated by the weather?"

Maybe your job is not more important than the janitor's, but it is more "meaningful," isn't it? Let's find out. Meaning is generally defined in the context of work as "satisfying an inner need."

"Does your work satisfy an *inner* need?" "Is your job something you do in order to be *fulfilled* as a human being?" "If so, what inner need does your work fulfill?" Be specific because perceiving one's work as a "calling," instead of a "job," is one of the few factors that significantly correlate to how satisfied you are with your work."[xii] Think about it. Do you have a "calling" or do you have a "job?"

Pencil in your answers to the above questions. You'll need them later.

If you are like most managers and employees to whom we have posed these questions, you may feel a clear, palpable level of discomfort about now. Most people, after a little thought, conclude that they have a job, not a calling, and that which they spend doing half their waking lives is neither important nor meaningful. For most, work does not fulfill an *inner* need, but rather it is simply a sacrifice of time and energy to meet *external* needs and wants.

> *I work in a small plant in Iowa out in the middle of a corn field. We stamp out plastic parts to make dashboards and other parts for cars. And, in answer to your question, "No, my job and my work are not 'important' and they are not 'meaningful.'" In the end, our work ends up in a junkyard or landfill somewhere crapping up the environment. If I had a choice—and I don't—I wouldn't do this again."*
>
> *- Greg, Department Manager, 2000*

Like Greg, you probably know the world will keep spinning on its axis if you choke on your pork chop tonight. You know that if you don't show up at work, whatever you did there will soon be absorbed by someone else in short order. You know that given enough money, you would do something else with your waking hours than the job you are doing today, and even though you may not know exactly what it is you would do, you have a nascent sense you'd be happy doing it.

A mentor of ours learned these lessons the hard way. Andy walked out of private law practice after 30 years, having built a $7 million a year book of business. We asked him, "When you called and told your largest corporate client that you were quitting, a client to whom you provided intimate advice at the highest levels for more than two decades, what did the CEO say to you?"

Andy thought for minute.

"The CEO said, 'Your absence will leave a large hole in our organization.'"

That was the long, but mostly the short, of their discussion. Andy recalled that the entire conversation lasted less than two minutes, and more tellingly, within a week the client had found and hired his replacement. Apparently, the hole Andy left wasn't so gaping that it couldn't be readily plugged. After making the transition to not working, we later asked Andy, "How would you summarize your professional career, one that took you to its very pinnacle?"

His reply was simple. "I made the rich richer," he said, a noticeable remorse in his voice.

So much for "meaning" in Andy's career. After a stint as CEO of a public corporation, Andy tossed in the towel and learned the rest of the lesson: he was happier not working.

Unless you are one of the relative handful of people whose work fulfills an *inner* need, what you do for a living boils down to putting bread on your table, clothes on your back, a roof over your head, and enough money to buy more stuff.

But aren't there employees who are truly passionate about their jobs, whose jobs satisfy inner needs, as opposed to the money and the stuff? Yes, there are, and we have had the opportunity of working with some of these people. You can recognize them by their answer to this question:

"Would you do the job you are doing today if there was no paycheck at all?"

Most managers and employees to whom we ask this question answer with a resounding, "No way!" They recognize, after giving it almost no thought, that they work for reasons *external* to themselves—most often money, stuff, power or prestige. A relative few answer, "Yes, I would do what I am doing, even if there was no paycheck, even if it meant doing it in my spare time." They are the few who have meaningful work.

Who are they? What is their work?

While it is hard to classify specific vocations as meaningful to the exclusion of others, we find those who enjoy meaningful work generally fall into one of three vocational categories: *Givers, Creators,* and *Visionaries.*

Let's take a brief look at each of these groups, and as we do, ask yourself, "Am I one of these?"

- *Givers: Healers, Protectors, and Educators.*

> *I was an engineer for a major electronics company. I hated every minute of it. Today, I teach high school math to gifted and talented students. Mine is a gift to them as I see them learn, grow, and understand. I make half as much money and get ten times as much enjoyment. I would never go back to corporate America.*
>
> *- Henry, Teacher*

As a teacher, Henry's passion for his work is defined by its long-term, life-changing impact on others. Religious leaders, teachers, professors, doctors, and nurses—those who nurture and heal our souls, minds, and bodies—often fall into this category of "healers, protectors, and educators," as do many police and fire personnel whose passion is to serve others. Similarly, we have met journalists who are so passionate about the truth, and judges who are so passionate about justice, that truth and justice are a part of their psyches, their value systems, and their vocations are a realization of a greater good.

29

Russ is a good example of a "Giver." He is a supervisory Emergency Medical Technician (EMT) in Fresno, California, and has been for 14 years. When we asked him, "What made you choose this field?" he replied, without hesitation, "I was taught from an early age that contentment and peace in life comes from serving others. I was an Eagle Scout and went into EMT as soon as I graduated from high school at 17. It was easy for me to choose a profession where blood and mayhem are the order of the day, making comparatively modest pay, because how better to be in service to others than saving lives, and I get to do that every day."

As to whether all EMT's were in the profession for the same reason, Russ haltingly replied, "No, not everyone. I find two types of people attracted to public service: those who want to serve and those who want power. I see the difference in the EMT's I supervise, in the police we work with regularly, and in all public sectors. In the end, it is both the profession and the person."

Just as all EMT's do not find "meaning" in their work, many teachers, doctors, and policemen don't, either. Some go into these professions for reasons other than the meaning they offer. But, if you are like Russ or Henry, whose purpose in life is to serve others, to teach others, to protect others, and have found a job that provides that opportunity to serve others, you are among the most fortunate people in the world of work and you need little from the workplace other than what your work provides.

- *Creators, Artists, and Discoverers*

> *I am a muralist. I have painted murals in New York and Maine and Michigan, and many here in Mexico. I am always painting in my mind, even when I sleep, and I can never wait for the time I can bring it all to life. I am poor, but I am blessed.*
>
> *- Jorge, San Miguel de Allende, Mexico*

For another fortunate few, like Jorge, work is the artistic expression of themselves. Many writers, poets, scientists, researchers, painters, sculptors, actors and musicians fall into this category. They go to work each day without giving much thought to money and the stuff it buys. If money comes, it comes. If it doesn't, and it most often doesn't, it wasn't the purpose of the experience in the first place.

The Creator's journey is one of expression, just as the scientist's is one of discovery. Einstein wasn't thinking about the bucks he would pocket from expounding the theory of relativity. Jackson Pollock wasn't imagining fame when he poured that first can of paint across a canvass. The guitar player who plays club dates for $250 a week, long ago having given up the dream of making best-selling records, doesn't show up at another smoky bar to play for drunks for any other reason than that making music is his passion. If you know a starving artist or musician, you understand.

- *Builders and Visionaries*

> *A young woman approached her employer to see if he'd like to back her in a new business endeavor. His response? "A cookie store is a bad idea. Besides, the market research reports say America likes crispy cookies, not soft and chewy cookies like you make." That woman was Debbi Fields (Mrs. Fields).*

Within the world of business, there are Builders and Visionaries who, like Debbie Fields, are characterized by their desire to do something different, relentlessly committed to making their visions their reality. No matter the hurdles and discouragement they experience, they cannot be dissuaded from their passions.

Football legend Vince Lombardi is another good example. He was told by one of his early coaches that he should forget about a career in coaching, saying he possessed only "minimal" football knowledge and lacked motivation. Walt Disney, the visionary for millions of children worldwide, was told by the editor of the newspaper where he worked that he should forget about a career in anything creative because he "totally lacked ideas."

Bill Gates at Microsoft and Jeff Bezos at Amazon.com are modern examples of those who visualize something new and different. And, they keep coming to work even when money is no longer an object. Their visions are extensions of themselves and their callings nurture them, cradle to grave.

Unlike EMT's, teachers, and starving artists, however, whose passions as *Givers* and *Creators* are easy to identify, genuine *Builders* and *Visionaries* are more difficult to spot. Like Bill Gates, they do exist, but there are far more impostors. Indeed, most executives with whom we have worked are not notably passionate about their work, but they are rather passionate about external success—either their own success, or their company's—which is almost always measured economically. While inner passion and passion for success are often mistaken, they are different.

Passion is something found inside, something profound, something essential, and something almost always creative or giving. Success, on the other hand, is almost always defined externally, is ego-driven, and is usually measured financially. We find plenty of successful people in corporate America, but few who have a vision that cannot be purchased for enough money.

How about you? Are you one of the handful in the American workplace who find inner meaning in your work, whose work expresses your identity? If so, give this book to one of the other 99% who haven't found their vocational passion, or if they did, they sacrificed it for a "better job" with bucks and benefits. If you work for a private sector company, association, or some branch of government, and you market, advertise, make, sell, insure, service, support, or regulate stuff, it may be hard to admit, but the *sine qua non* of you dragging yourself to work each day is something *other* than your soul-fed loving passion for the "meaningful" work you do.

The Death of Meaningful Work

Was there a time when more work had more meaning? Yes.

Before the Industrial Revolution, before the division of labor, before the scientific method of production, there were more Creators—people whose work was their art. You can still find the remnants of that time today in the Third World, where industry has yet dominated all design and production of stuff. There remain many Creators there—artisans whose work is in stark contrast to their counterparts in the industrialized world.

In the high desert of central Mexico, for example, villagers trek to Patzcuaro on Fridays for market. Colorful blankets, hand tooled copper and lacquered wood items are designed, crafted, and brought to the market for sale. Each village in that area has a particular craft for which it is known, a craft that has been passed down from one generation to the next for

31

centuries. The villagers from Santa Clara del Cobre, for example, specialize in copper vessels—hand made, each pounded from a single piece of copper. From cups to kitchen sinks, each is designed, crafted, and sold by its Creator at the weekly market.

Contrast this villager, this craftsman, this Creator, to the machine operator in a typical plastics factory who watches temperature and pressure gauges as tens of thousands of cups are extruded daily—cups which the machine operator did not create, design, craft, or sell. Rather, he just watches gauges and most likely the time clock, too. So what is the difference? They both, after all, make cups. Yet, there are both quantitative and qualitative differences. In the case of the machine operator, he can make thousands of cups each day, while the artisan in central Mexico may make one or two. Qualitatively, the artisan's work is artistic, creative, and complete, from design to manufacture to marketing, while the job of the modern extruder operator involves little, if any, creativity. The craftsman knows he is an artist, a Creator. The machine operator knows what he is, too—a "human resource," feeding a giant "machine resource."

Add the time clock, which tells workers when to do what they do, and mass production, which minimizes individual skills needed to get it done, and you can see that modernity has stripped most work of its "meaning."

> *I'm in my early 40s, manage nearly 50 employees, yet I already have ulcers, severe migraines, and heart arrhythmia, mostly from trying to get things done with corporate bureaucrats standing in my way, or better said, sitting in my way. I have a college degree, but sometimes I want to return to the time clock and forget trying to get the most out of human beings at any cost.*

> *- Jim, Supervisor*

Like most first-line supervisors with whom we work, Jim knows his work isn't meaningful. It wasn't designed to be meaningful. Jim's job as a supervisor in a factory was engineered to be efficient, cost-effective, and productive. Jim is judged and rewarded solely on his ability to produce more widgets at less cost. The not-so-subtle bargain for Jim's services is simple and straightforward: "If you get more work out of fewer people, you get to keep your job and you may get promoted, which will mean more money, more stuff, and perhaps an early ticket out of here. If you don't, we'll find someone who can."

Jim knows that if his job, or the jobs of those whom he manages, could be done by a machine, they would be done by a machine, and it is only a lack of available technology that his job is not being done by a machine. He also knows that the day may come when the widgets made in his factory are "outsourced" or "offshored," and that his company would do either at the drop of hat if it meant another dime in quarterly earnings.

Now, consider your job. Do you believe that whoever designed your job had, as a primary consideration, the creation of "meaningful work" for you? Work that, without more, is enjoyable, personally rewarding, and internally significant?

We'll help you with the answer to that question. The answer is "No."

The designers of your job, like the designers of most jobs, broke big tasks into smaller tasks, and smaller tasks into even smaller tasks, then designed your job around one or more of those tasks. The designers of your job did not take into account the impact of the division of labor on you, your employees, your fellow workers, your family, your friends, your time, your health, or your happiness. It is why today's workplace induces unhappiness, boredom, monotony, fatigue, anxiety, accidents, stress, mental instability, and even violence.[xiii] It is why most Americans are no longer "reasonably satisfied" with their work or their jobs.

Meaningful Work: No Turning Back the Hands Of Time

Can we put meaning back into work? Yes.

Will we put meaning back into work? No.

To put "meaning" back into work would require a radical paradigm shift, one in which the product of work was not efficiency, profit, and money, but rather "meaning" - on meeting the inner needs of workers. For good or ill, few people would willingly sacrifice modern conveniences and the stuff to which they have become accustomed for the amorphous promise of a "meaning" they have never experienced or even know exists.

In factories and offices all over the United States, we have found employees stamping out plastic parts, working in brick ovens, loading baggage on busses, correcting lines of computer code, selling cars, cleaning toilets, taking orders from customers, listening to the whining of clients, and negotiating the best deals. But we have found few employees who deem their work "meaningful," or would go to their job tomorrow if given enough money to do something else.

To the contrary, most employees believe their work to be mind-numbing and repetitive, divided into ever smaller tasks so that the whole can no longer be seen or understood. Employees see little, if any, long-term positive impact on society or themselves resulting from their work. They know it is true and they are diminished by it,[xiv] leaving most employees still in search of a reason to go to work each day that will make them happy.

What about you?

CHAPTER 4

The Myth of Too Much Time

"My work? Meaningful? Ha! Not even close. I am a supervisor in an accounting department for a commercial bank. We crunch numbers, hardly world-saving efforts. Why do I do it? Well, the paycheck is the primary reason, and I do like the people I work with, but I often think that if I had enough money I'd probably still come to work. Crazy, isn't it, but if I didn't have this job to come to each day, what else would I do? I'd probably just end up in trouble."

- Bill, Accounting Manager

LIKE Bill, would you continue showing up for work each day if you had enough money to do something else? Can you think of something you'd rather do than your job? Would you be bored if you didn't have your job to do each day? Would you fear becoming a "couch potato," becoming dull and useless, unneeded and unwanted? Does work, as Voltaire cautioned, "spare us from three evils: boredom, vice, and need?"

Think about it. Imagine for a moment that you had a million dollars. What would you do tomorrow? Could you fill your days with interesting, meaningful pursuits? Before answering, we'll ask just one favor—don't engage in the fantasy that you would sit on a beach everyday and sip Piña Coladas for the rest of your days and be happy. You wouldn't. Instead, you would become a bored, sunburned, unhappy drunk. Nor would you snow ski everyday if you lived on the slopes. You would get tired of recreation, because all banal enjoyments lose their allure. You would do *something*.

The question is this: What would you do?

Like Bill, would you show up tomorrow at work because it is all you know to do? Have you spent your entire life preparing for work and then working to the exclusion of other, perhaps more meaningful, pursuits? Like Bill, would you wonder what you would do if you had no place to go in the morning—no computer, no keyboard, and no spreadsheet to recalculate a dozen times each day? Does the thought of giving up your job to do something else frighten you?

Do you believe, like Bill, that you would "get into trouble" if you had too much time on your hands and nothing to do with that time? Do you believe that idle hands are, indeed, the "devil's workshop"? Without your work, would you end up eating bon-bons while you watch daytime television, or would you fall into hideous addictions because there are not widgets to be stamped out, customers to be calmed, or employees to be managed? Would you die with your face in the soup, having fallen asleep on life, if you stopped working tomorrow? Would you end up robbing liquor stores if you didn't put on your tie and go downtown each morning?

If you believe you would, you suffer from the *Myth of Too Much Time*—the argument for work by default, *i.e.,* Work doesn't have to be meaningful. It just has to *be.* Work is what you prepared to do with your life. Work is all there is. Work is all there ever will be.

Many employees and managers we talk to believe, or act like they believe, there is nothing in life except work, and that boredom is the natural result of not working. We will include one manager we had in a seminar a few years ago. His name is Rob, and he was a top efficiency consultant. Rob's job was to make workplaces more efficient, more productive—euphemisms for getting more work out of fewer people and thereby putting more money into the shareholders' pockets. He was a great technician with a compelling personality, made a lot of money, but came to despise his work. Like many execs we know, Rob spent too many nights with his business plans and too few at home with his family and friends. He spent too much time thinking about money and too little thinking about people. Even within his own company, he was looked at more like a highly efficient machine than a human being.

Yet he recalls on reflection, "I was supposed to be happy. I had it all. But I wasn't happy, which left me feeling guilty and looking for a reason to continue showing up at work every day." Rob found his reason in the *Myth of Too Much Time*—the belief that he had to continue doing what he was doing because he had nothing else to do. "After all," Rob told us, "I had not been trained to do anything else. I was good at what I did. I had no passions to do anything else, probably because I was too busy working to search for passion." His logic, however strained, provided him enough reason to continue wearing the blinders and plowing the row. In our training session, Rob concluded for all to hear, "My work sucks!" and in the next breath argued that if it were not for his work, he would be lost, would have nothing to do, would get bored, and would be unhappy, ignoring, of course, that he was already unhappy.

A year later, by happenstance, we had an opportunity to visit with Rob again and asked how he was progressing. He smiled. "I quit my job six months ago."

We thought he was joking.

"I'm serious," he said. And, through an eerie calm which was in deep contrast to the hyper-active Rob we had met in our class, we knew he'd pulled the trigger. It seems that, without warning, he walked away from his six-figure income and a high-rise office suite for something else.

"It happened last New Year's Eve," he began. "I looked out my office window and saw thousands of lights still burning in office buildings all over the city. I was one of those lights. I always thought I was different, somehow, but it was then I recognized that I was a part of the same herd that made their way downtown each day to jobs they didn't like very much."

"So," he continued, "I took off my tie and laid it on my desk. I took the pictures of my kids, and left everything else. It was time to find out whether work was an essential component of my life. I was fortunate. I had the million dollars you guys talked about. The only question was whether I could survive without the daily grind. Did I have to do my job to avoid boredom? Was there something else out there for me? Could I find something I really loved to do, something for which I had passion? I decided I had to know whether happiness might lie at the end of an unmarked road, one that didn't take me to any particular place at any particular time. I had to know if life could be lived without a day-planner."

He smiled. "It can and I am," Rob said confidently. "I call what I have done 'voluntary simplicity,' and since I left the world of work, life has been a series of trade-offs. Today I wear Old Navy, not Armani; I live in a condo instead of a 5,000 square-foot house; I drive a used Toyota instead of a new Lexus."

"In exchange, I live without an alarm clock, because I have few external time demands. My life is a series of moments, one after another, present moments, my moments. I don't live in the past, always worrying about some mistake I might have made, nor do I live in the future–that time where fear and worry will ruin your life if given a chance. Instead, I wake up each day and decide what it is I want to do with that day—the next 24 hours."

He took out a pen and began to scribble on a cocktail napkin. "Here's the way my life works now. I get ten hours of sleep a day, eight at night, and a two-hour nap most afternoons. It's civilized," he said, no apology. "That leaves 14 hours. I read for two hours. I found out that I love to read. That leaves 12 hours. I workout, play basketball, and take a steam. That is another two hours. So, I'm left with 10 more hours each day. I journal, write personal correspondence, telephone my friends, and surf the web. That's another two hours a day, leaving only 8 more hours. I eat three times a day, and I don't mean stuffing a McSomething in my face over a stack of papers on a desk I can't see for the clutter. I mean I now prepare and enjoy my food, something I had never done before. That's another two hours a day, which leaves 6 hours. I have three kids from my prior marriage, and it seems I inadvertently missed most of their childhoods while selling my previous life away in tenth-hour increments to the highest bidder." His voice turned momentarily bitter. "An hour or two a day for them wouldn't be too much to ask, would it?" he asked, rhetorically.

"So what time remains? Four or five hours each day, and I now spend several hours a week working at the local children's hospital. I find I do have a passion after all: a passion to help children who are ill. I go and read to them three times a week. It's the best part of my week!" he exclaimed. "I never knew I had that passion, and never would have known, but for my decision about work."

"Now, what's left?" he asked. "Precious little time to read the paper at Starbucks, go to the bookstore, the library, and the corner bar, enjoy a glass of wine on my little patio with a friend, go to the grocery store, get my hair cut, play my guitar, pay the rent, or take an evening walk with someone who cares nothing of my ambition—of who I once was—but only of me."

He shook his head. "You were right, fellows. The *Myth of Too Much Time* is just that— a myth. There isn't too much time; there is too little time. I use up 24 hours every day, never work, and still have choices to make about what will fit in my life and what will not."

How does Rob's story make you feel? Does it make you want to unknot your tie, lay it on your desk, and walk into a world without work or into a life with work that has meaning? If you don't have a passion for your work, if your work is not meaningful, those are the questions you should be asking yourself right now. Could you, like Rob, fill the time you have remaining with activities more pleasurable than your work? Most managers, after giving it some thought, tell us they not only could fill the time they spend working do other things, but would fill that time with activities other than their current jobs.

With the *Myths of Meaningful Work* and *Too Much Time* no longer available to justify the work performed by most people, we are left with the perplexing question, "Why do we spend half of our waking lives working at jobs we don't like?" Money and the stuff it buys, of course, which brings us to the most common and most powerful of all the myths of work— the *Myth of More*.

CHAPTER 5

The Myth of More

"My job is a mind-numbing 60 hour-a-week marathon spent faking enthusiasm for things that don't matter. I thought what I did was really important until my husband was stricken with cancer. It was only then that I reflected on my work and wondered, "Why? Why did I spend so much time and emotional capital on my job?" It didn't take me long to come up with the answer. It was the money, of course. I never thought of myself as materialistic; cars, jewelry, and clothes have never been very important to me. But, over the years I have accumulated stuff—bigger, better, and more stuff. I found it impossible to escape the trap of identifying with what I owned because that is the way others identified me. So, I worked and spent and worked some more just like all the rest."

- Carolyn, Vice President of Administration

CAROLYN is typical. Money and stuff was the reason she worked and, indeed, most people work. Work is just the *means* most of us utilize to get to the *end* of accumulation. Why? Because most Americans believe that *quantity of stuff equals quality of life.*

This symbol is the zeitgeist of western culture.

Stuff and Its Relationship To Work

Stop for a moment. Look around at all the stuff you have today and the stuff you don't have today but want tomorrow, the stuff you see on TV, the Internet, and in the mall. Make two lists. Call the first one "My Stuff." This is stuff you already have. Then make another list called "Stuff I Want," which is stuff you don't have yet, but you believe would make your life better or happier. Take a close look at the first list—the stuff you have. This list contains all the reward most people have garnered from their first job to the job they currently hold. Now, take a look at your second list. This is what you are willing to sacrifice your time for in order to accumulate. These are the reasons most people have worked, are working, and will work in the future, even at jobs they do not find "reasonably satisfying."

Stuff is that powerful. It is stuff that causes punch-presses to punch, telephones to be answered, letters to be typed, customers to be satisfied, and toilets to be cleaned. In our seminars, the most common answer to the question, "Why do you work?" is "Because I want *more* for me and my family." They rarely say "more" what, but "more stuff" is what they mean.

It is an answer that is both sad and ironic, if only because stuff never seems to satisfy us for very long. Why? Because once we transfer stuff from the "Stuff I Want" to the "My Stuff" list, we create a void and we need to fill it with another piece of stuff we want, thus preventing our existing stuff from ever become *enough* stuff for very long. And so, we have to work harder and longer to make more money to buy more stuff. It is like climbing a mountain. We climb one step at a time, and after multiple assaults on the summit, we finally succeed. We have arrived! We cheer ourselves, only to discover that the top of what we thought was the mountain is not the top of the mountain at all, but just a plateau that is the bottom of another mountain. So we begin climbing again and reach the top, only to find another plateau, and still another. The same is true with money and the stuff it buys. We work, earn, and buy more stuff, believe for a moment that it is finally enough stuff, only to discover there is more stuff to be bought. We work harder, longer, and at jobs that may provide us little or no satisfaction, hoping against hope that the next stuff we buy will be enough stuff. And sure enough, it isn't.

Repeat cycle until death.

Welcome to the *Myth of More*, the pervasive, strongly-held belief that work will one day provide us with enough stuff. A good example of the *Myth of More* in action is our homes.

Measuring Our Success By The Square Foot

During the last 25 years, the average American house has grown from 1,660 square feet to 2,200 square feet, a 25 percent increase in the amount of space in which we eat, sleep, but mostly watch television (seven hours a day on average) on one of several sets.[xv] We don't seem to notice the irony associated with building bigger houses, even though we spend less time in them, in large part because we're working harder to pay for them.[xvi]

Yet no matter how many square feet we wall off from the world, there is always more that can be bricked in, and as a society we don't seem embarrassed in the least about our desire for bigger and better when it comes to our personal living space.[xvii]

Money, itself, is another example. Can there ever be *enough* money in your bank account, since there is always room for *more* money? Can there be enough cars in your garage, since there is always room for another car, and if not, there is always room for another garage. Regardless of the number of cars in your garage or the number of garages you have in which to store them, there can always be more expensive cars inside these garages. The game is played at all levels, whether you're stepping up from a Chevy to a Buick, or whether you've stepped up to one of the 17 ultra-luxury model automobiles for sale in the United States with base retail prices exceeding $100,000. As long as there is stuff out there that we do not possess, most of us continue playing the game—wanting, working, buying, having, wanting more—and repeating the cycle, never consciously saying, "This is it. This is enough." And believing it!

Why do we play this game that we cannot win? Because we believe, even in the face of overwhelming, objective evidence to the contrary that more eventually has to become enough. We think the relationship of "more" and "enough" as if we were filling a glass with milk. At some point, more milk becomes enough milk because the glass is full. There is no more room for more milk. Yet the analogy fails when it comes to money and stuff, because the glass into which we pour more money and more stuff expands each time we add to it, causing whatever money we have already poured into the glass to never quite fill it. It is the expanding nature of our desires that keeps more from becoming enough, thus keeping us in a state of struggle.

The *Myth of More* is so powerful that it keeps people working at jobs with little or no meaning, and in many cases, working at jobs they actively dislike. Asked what factor would most improve the quality of their lives, the most common answer by Americans is "more money."[xviii] In fact, we are so hooked on "more" as the endgame of personal happiness that we not only select our work and jobs based on how much they pay, but even our spouses. One survey finds that women consider "earning power" the most important single characteristic when evaluating potential mates. Men are not much different, rating earning power second, only behind physical attractiveness.[xix]

How Much More Is Enough For You?

Let's forget for a moment the premise that more won't lead to enough. That shouldn't be hard, because most of us have a number, an amount of money in mind that we believe would be *both* more and enough, that would satisfy us for the rest of our lives. What is your number?

Don't lie. Not to yourself. If you doubled your disposable income, would that be enough? Would a million dollars be enough? Regardless of how you define "*enough*," define it now. Be specific. Write the number down.

Do you need some help? Read these phrases out loud and see if any feel like "enough":

- "I'd be satisfied forever if my salary was doubled."
- "I'd be satisfied forever if my portfolio gained 20 percent every year."
- "I'd be satisfied forever if my 401(k) was 50 percent larger.
- "I'd be satisfied forever if I inherited two million dollars."

Did any of those feel right to you?

If you still have a hard time coming up with your number, shoot high. If you won the lottery, would that be *enough*? Would that make you happy? If you were fingering the winning ticket right now, how would you feel? Wouldn't you be giddy if you knew that all you had to do to increase your net worth by $10 million was catch a flight to your state lottery headquarters? Sure you would. We all would.

More, Enough and Time

Now that you have your number, ask yourself, "If I had that much money, how *long* would it remain *enough* money? How long would it keep me satisfied, happy, ecstatic, overjoyed, elated, blissful, or if none of those work for you, insert your own adjective.

It is a good question. You should know the answer, and come to peace with the answer, because knowing just how long more money and more stuff remains enough, and thus keeps us satisfied, will make your life better.

The answer? Whatever number you wrote down would remain "enough" and keep you satisfied for about 6 months to 1 year. That is how long it takes for the euphoria of more money and more stuff to wear off. After that, you would be on the hunt again, looking for more in order to chase the high that had worn off.

Don't take our word for it. Psychologists, economists, and other social scientists have spent entire lifetimes studying the relationship of money, happiness, and time. They have studied those who have money, those who don't have money, those who once had money and lost their money, those who are poor but believe they are rich and those who are rich but believe they are poor. They have compared, contrasted, poked, surveyed, studied, prodded, and measured. What's their conclusion? There are several, actually, and you should know them all:

- Once the basic needs of food, shelter, and clothing are met, there is *no correlation* between more money and long-term happiness. None.[xx]
- Those whose incomes have increased over a 10-year period are not happier than those whose income has not increased over the same period.[xxi]
- Events such as being promoted have little effect on people's moods after 3 months, and no trace after 6 months.[xxii]
- Those who completed PhDs are no happier than those who completed the 8th grade. [xxiii]
- Those who take the bus to work in overalls are just as happy as those who wear suits and drive to work in fancy cars.[xiv]
- Most lottery winners are no happier a year after they win the lottery than they were the day before they won the lottery.[xxv] (This is not to say lottery winners don't get a jolt of joy from their winnings. They do. But their euphoria doesn't last. "In the long run, neither an ice cream cone nor a new car, nor becoming rich and famous produces the same feelings of delight that it initially did... Happiness is not the result of being rich, but a *temporary consequence* of having recently become richer.") [xxvi]
- "Only recent life events seem to influence a person's well-being, and this effect drops off very quickly"—that is, in about three months.[xxvii]
- Long-term happiness is not dictated by sudden tragedy or wealth. Studies of both lottery winners and paraplegics illustrate that within a year after these events that bring great joy or sadness, happiness levels return to their pre-event levels.[xxviii]
- More money isn't the dictating factor in what is known as our "subjective happiness quotient," that is, how happy we feel for more than a few months.[xxix]

Like it or not, those are the facts. No salary increase, bonus, promotion, or even winning the lottery will make "more" become "enough" and thus keep you satisfied for more than one year. Before you protest, you are not "different" than all the rest. You are the same, because you are human and so are your employees and your co-workers and your family.[xxx]

If you don't believe it, use your own experience with people you know as the litmus test. Write down the names of the three people you know who have the most money—not acquaintances, but people you really know. Now take the three people with the least money whom you know (assuming they have their basic needs met: food, clothing, shelter, and basic education). Now, order them by how happy they seem to be—not how happy you think they *should* be, but how happy they are, based on your objective observations. If you're like most managers with whom we work, you will find no correlation between a person's money and their happiness.

The unhealthy relationship with money, or better said, unrealistic beliefs of what money can provide and what it cannot provide and for how long, is in large part why job satisfaction in the United States did not increase between 1972 and 1991, despite an increase of 39 percent in net pay (adjusted for inflation), and why since then, job satisfaction has decreased precipitously. This relationship is at least in part responsible for the increasing rates of depression and suicide in most Western countries, especially richer nations like the United States.

Why Doesn't More Become Enough?

While most experts studying the relationship between money and happiness agree that there is little, if any, relationship between "more" and "enough" once basic needs have been met, yet there are differences of opinion as to why that is so. Here are three compelling theories:

(1) Habituation

Human beings are, if nothing else, adaptable. We "go with the flow." We are a species that naturally habituates, meaning that we adapt to differing circumstances—rich or poor, sick or healthy. Some contend that it is our ability to adapt that has caused humans as a species to survive and flourish.

But it is also the reason more does not, and cannot, become enough, at least not for very long. In a matter of months, after an event—any event—we learn to accept the consequences of that event, whether those consequences are good, bad or indifferent. Dr. David Lykken in *Happiness—The Nature and Nurture Of Joy and Contentment,* describes the phenomenon this way:

> *People who had suffered some misfortune within recent weeks turned out to have lower scores on subjective well-being. Those who had experienced cheering, happy-making events recently were happier than average. But if the good or bad experiences were as far removed as three months back, their effects on present mood were nearly impossible to distinguish and, if as long as six months earlier, no residual effects were visible."*[xxxi]
>
> *Like most mammals, ours is a remarkably adaptable or accommodating or habituating species... People who have been devastated by the loss of a loved one often feel a guilty surprise to find, six months later, that they can smile and enjoy life again. People who have suffered crippling and permanent injures typically recover*

psychologically quicker than we luckier ones would have believed possible... We "get over" or adapt to success and good fortune just as readily."[xxxii]

Others who have studied human happiness similarly opine that the half-life of happiness generated by more money and the stuff it buys is short, usually six months, and almost never more than one year. We simply get used to the hand we are dealt, whether it is good, bad, or indifferent.

Christopher Reeve is a good example. Within one year of his catastrophic accident that rendered him a quadriplegic, he said was able to find joy again. And, just as Reeve retraced to his prior level of happiness, lottery winners do the same in about the same length of time.

(2) Comparison

Other experts believe that it is not so much our ability to habituate that takes the staying power out of more, but our ability to compare what we have with what others have that keeps us from having a permanent smile on our faces when we are presented with more money or more stuff. Our "satisfaction depends, not on absolute levels of consumption, but on one's level *relative* to others, [so] no matter how much you possess, you won't feel well off if Jones next door suddenly possesses more."[xxxiii] In other words, more remains enough only until we look around and compare ourselves with a new reference group. Once the comparison is made, more is no longer more. It is simply where we are, and then we need another reference point.[xxxiv]

You know the feeling. You get a pay raise. You buy a new car or house. You wonder how you ever lived on your previous income, lived in that small house, or drove that old car. Why? Experts tell us it is because we are quick to raise the bar of comparison to our new income level; that is, from every vantage point, no matter how high, there is someone with more, and once you achieve a higher income level, you begin comparing your money and stuff with those who are at a similar income level. Thus the enjoyment we experience from more money and the things it buys is limited to the time it takes to reposition the bar.

This comparative theory of monetary-based happiness was observed by Eric Fromm who, in his classic work, *The Sane Society*, described the phenomenon of comparative wealth in a materialistic society:

Modern man, if he dared to be articulate about his concept of heaven, would describe a vision which would look like the biggest department store in the world, showing new things and gadgets, and himself having plenty of money with which to buy them. He would wander around open-mouthed in this heaven of gadgets and commodities, provided only that there were ever more and newer things to buy, and perhaps that his neighbors were just a little less privileged than he.[xxxv]

The comparisons we make with others are, incidentally, why across-the-board financial incentives granted by most companies do not have the intended effect, if the intended effect is employee satisfaction. If the pleasure brought by increased wealth is comparative, then if everyone in the office gets a raise, no one

43

is in a *comparatively* better position, thus taking the joy out of having more in relation to anyone else.[xxxvi]

If the happiness we feel upon attaining more diminishes because our reference point changes, then it would also follow that happiness might turn to sadness or despair if the bar of comparison is raised while our income is not. According to Juliet Schor, that is exactly what happens. In *The Overspent American,* Schor observes that when comparisons of income and wealth are made with friends down the street, we stay generally satisfied—not elated, but not actively unhappy either. It makes sense. Most people on the same block live in nearly equivalent houses and drive similar cars and have similar toys, and while everyone is more or less has equal stuff, we may not be ecstatic, but we are not unhappy, either. When we gain more through a big raise or promotion, we move out of our neighborhood and into a new one and begin comparing ourselves with those who share the stuff of our new means. After about six months, that becomes the norm and our happiness level recedes to its original position.

Moreover, Schor contends that if we begin comparing ourselves to people outside our neighborhood, perhaps fictional people, such as our "Friends" on television—people who appear to work at ordinary jobs like we do but who live far better than we do—we can make ourselves unhappy. Comparisons that are irrational can turn our dreams into nightmares.

(3) Genetics

Still others who have studied the relationship of money, happiness, and time contend that the failure of more to satisfy us over the long term is not adaptive or comparative, but rather is determined genetically. These researchers contend that each of us has a pre-determined level of happiness, and that we return to that level after both good events and bad.

Dr. David Lykken tested this theory by determining whether monozygotic (identical) twins separated at birth were more similar in their reported happiness than, say, same-sex fraternal twins raised together—those who share only half their genes.[xxxvii] His conclusion after this remarkable study was that "trying to be happier is like trying to be taller,"[xxxviii] finding that identical twins that grew up in wholly different environments were about equally happy or unhappy. Yet, even those who, like Lykken, subscribe to what is known as the "happiness set-point theory," acknowledge that a person's happiness set-point can be raised or lowered, but that it cannot be bought, finding no "appreciable correlation between happiness and social status or income."[xxxix] To the contrary, there is some evidence that those who pin happiness on wealth are, indeed, less happy than those who find happiness elsewhere,[xl] in part because wealth "serves to add layer upon layer of complexity to one's life."[xli]

Putting this theory into modern context, Geoffrey Miller observed that "Popular culture is dominated by advertisements that offer the following promise: buy our goods or service, and your subjective well-being will increase. The happiness research demonstrates that most of such promises are empty. Perhaps all advertisements for non-essential goods should be required to carry the warning: 'Caution: Scientific research demonstrates that this product will increase your subjective well-being only in the short term, if at all, and will not increase your happiness set-point.'"[xlii]

Bottom line: "Your next raise or promotion will be both more and enough" is an insidious, yet endemic, lie. Material desires are insatiable. We will never be happier at work if more-money and more stuff are the only reasons we are there.

Knowing this leaves us at a crossroads. We can continue believing the *Myth of More,* running like rats in a rolling cage, faster and faster, knowing that we're going nowhere, or we can acknowledge that the "want-work-spend-want more" cycle is a desperate, and ultimately doomed, attempt to buy a ticket on the *Streetcar Named Enough,* a train that seems always to have just left the station a few minutes before we arrived, and look for other opportunities the workplace provides to achieve satisfaction over the long haul.

PART III

"Real Life," "Work Life," All of Life: What Satisfies Us?

CHAPTER 6

If Not Meaning, More, or Time, Which Way To Nirvana?

"I remember when one of my employees, Juan, returned to Mexico to visit a sick relative. He left his wife, Lupita, and his two children, Jose and Alberto, here. He had problems trying to reenter the U.S. and it wasn't long before Lupita and the children were in desperate straits—no food, no rent money—even their electricity had been cut off. Lupita spoke no English, had no support system, and no friends. The company offered no help, so we took up a collection among my crew. I gave $400 out of my own pocket, and we took turns going by her place each day to make sure she and the kids were doing OK. By getting to know his family, I got to know Juan, because I learned what was most important in his life. Since this event, he's not just another employee. We care about each other as people, and that makes his job better—and mine, too."

- Jim, first-line manufacturing manager

WHILE more than half of all employees are not "reasonably satisfied" with their work, nearly half are. Yet, as we have observed, only a relative handful of those "reasonably satisfied" have "meaningful" work—that is, work that fulfills an inner need. How can that be? Who are these people?

Perhaps the largest group of those "reasonably satisfied" is comprised of those still chasing the American Dream: living within the *Myth of More*. And, they remain reasonably satisfied with their work until the day comes when they awaken and discover that more never becomes enough. Others are mired in self-importance, mistaking what someone will pay them to do their job with their personal worth. Until the day comes (and it usually does) that they are no longer of use to an employer as a "human resource," they may remain "reasonably satisfied" by believing the *Myth of Meaningful Work*.

Others bifurcate one life into two lives: a "real life" and a "work life." The first is the life from which they garner the most happiness, and the latter is merely the cost of the former. They do not believe work is supposed to contribute to life satisfaction, and so, if they are generally satisfied with life outside their work, they answer both questions (home life and work life) from that combined perspective. As we discussed in Chapter 5, still others are genetically predisposed to be reasonably satisfied, no matter what their circumstance.

Others conclude their work is "reasonably satisfying" because their lives away from work are so dysfunctional and unhappy that work, however unfulfilling, provides a temporal and physical escape. On a comparative basis, these employees will answer that they are "reasonably satisfied" with their work.

Perhaps the most interesting group are those who are reasonably satisfied with their work for reasons that have nothing to do with the work itself, nothing to do with more money or stuff, and nothing to do with perceived self-importance, self-deception, or mythology. Who are they? Jim, our first-line manufacturing manager who began this chapter, discovered the answer, and you can, too.

Let's begin with a hypothetical situation. Assume you don't work anymore. You don't have a mortgage or rent, utilities, a payment on your F-150 or BMW, and the expenses of keeping up the pool are no problem. Satisfying your Home Shopping Network obsession comes easy, as does paying your credit card bills. You're comfortable.

What would you do with your time?

We have asked hundreds of managers this question and most respond along these lines:

- "I would spend more time with people who mean the most to me—my family and my friends."
- "I would travel with my wife/husband/companion and see the world."
- "I would take my kids to school and pick them up each day."
- "I would make my little girl's soccer games—all of them."
- "I would spend more time in the backyard, playing catch with my son."
- "I would take a couple of hours each morning to discuss the things that really matter with my family."
- "I would spend leisurely time on the golf course or the tennis court with my friends."
- "I would get to know my neighbors."
- "I would help others."
- "I would involve myself in my community, neighborhood, and schools."

Are your answers consistent with these? What do these answers have in common?

Some have been fortunate to actually do what they would do if they didn't have to work. Some got rich and quit like our friend Rob in Chapter 4, who discovered the *Myth of Too Much Time* was just that—a myth. Others, like Pat Irelan, once had money, but discovered the *Myth Of More* didn't make him happy and chose to live without many things money can buy. Instead, he is a school crossing guard, a quantum leap from the limousines and servants that were once found on the 460-acre estate upon which he grew up. He gets along on his social security check, lives in subsidized housing, and doesn't own a car. A dozen times a year he plays Ebenezer Scrooge in Charles Dickens' "A Christmas Carol" in his hometown of Waynesville, Ohio. Asked why, he says, "I have learned people are so wrong when they believe happiness comes from materialism. All my life, I have heard people fight, feud and lie about money... and I just became nauseated by it."[xliii] Pat saw through the *Myth of More* and acted upon what he saw, jumped off the treadmill, and finds his joy in service to others.

Pat is not alone. An astonishing number of *Healers and Protectors* once chased the buck, found their lives lacking, and made transitions into new careers where their focus was shifted from money and stuff. Remember Henry, who left the engineering job in corporate

America to teach gifted and talented students in high school? He is happier now in service to his students than he ever was when he was programming computers.

Molly is another good example. After experiencing the pain associated with the lingering death of her mother, she has now gone from marketing fine jewelry to becoming a hospice worker, comforting the dying. Both Hank and Molly made the decision to serve others. Both are happy they did.

Others make remarkable career changes after significant emotional events in their lives. Maurice Matsumori was just a few feet from the World Trade Center when it collapsed. After watching people jump to their deaths and wondering whether they had died doing the jobs they loved, he made a decision to quit his high-paying job as a quality-control specialist, all because he experienced "the biggest wake-up call of my life."[xliv]

Marcy Scott Lynn followed in the same footsteps, quitting her job as a corporate-communications manager two weeks after the September 11 attacks, saying "I don't want to die wishing I had done something that meant more."[xlv] For both Maurice and Marcy, epiphanies led them to teaching—a place meaningful work can be found, a place where caring relationships are common.

Still others have left the workplace for avocations after they come to the conclusion that more will never become enough until they finally say, "Enough!" They discovered that the hedonistic, self-ingratiating, shop-till-you-drop lifestyles provided them with little joy after they habituated. Many who were born with, earned, or otherwise had the silver spoon firmly planted in their mouths have given up on trying to find happiness by jetting from one exotic destination to another, and they have refocused their lives on family, friends, community, and service to others.

Todd Wagner is a good example. He, along with his college buddy Mark Cuban, founded Broadcast.com in September of 1995 after quitting his job as a partner at one of the top law firms in Dallas, Texas. Broadcast.com was eventually sold to Yahoo four years later, netting Wagner and Cuban a cool $6 billion. Cuban went on to buy the Dallas Mavericks professional basketball team and a $12 million jet, among a plethora of other toys, including his own reality TV show.

Wagner took a different route, focusing his energy on service to others via community involvement, creating the Todd R. Wagner Foundation, whose primary mission is to bridge the "digital divide" that exists between the rich and the poor, providing capital for minority high-tech businesses. But he does more than write a check, devoting a great deal of his time to mentoring the owners of these businesses, believing the Internet can be a catalyst to change the fortunes of the financially disadvantaged. And making that possible is making Wagner happy. One close friend of Wagner observed, "It was a very tough choice (choosing between his ethos of philanthropy and the COO position offered to him by Yahoo). But Wagner made his decision, and he seems happier for it.[xlvi] He is a fortunate man, not because he is rich, but for the same reason that Hank the teacher, Molly the hospice worker, and Jim the first-line manufacturing manager, are fortunate. They, along with many who have studied happiness in the workplace, have discovered an important dynamic of life that most of us never learn.

It is caring, compassionate relationships with others, relationships based on giving, not getting, that make us happy over the long haul.[xlvii]

Most of us never understand that concept, because most of us never experience a moment when money is no longer an issue, as Todd Wagner experienced when he became wealthy, or Pat Irelan experienced when he decided that enough was enough. Sadly, most of us have deprived ourselves of seeing any color other than green in life's richly hued spectrum. We remain hypnotized by the *Myth Of More* that keeps us struggling for more money to buy more stuff— the gimcracks and gadgets and goodies of life—until we take our final unfulfilled breaths.

The young Turks of Wall Street are good examples of where the struggle for more leads. They are high-powered stock brokers in New York between the ages 22 and 32 and earn an average of $139,346 a year. Researchers studied a group employed by Wall Street's most prestigious firms and found that 23 percent of them evidenced major depression— three times the national average. Ironically, those with the most significant symptoms of depression, anxiety, emotional exhaustion and poor coping skills were those who made the *most* money, who were ostensibly the most "successful." Likewise, practicing law is now the highest-paid profession in the country, yet a high percentage of lawyers are depressed and unhappy, leading to a high turnover within that profession, many lawyers leaving the law for other vocations that pay less but provide more meaning.

The Quid Pro Quo: Your Choice

The *quid pro quo* for traditional "success", to include huge homes, fancy cars and big bank accounts has been their mental health, quality of life, and personal happiness The question is, "Is it worth it?"

You don't need to answer that question, because you've already answered it. Go back to the exercise—the hypothetical that began this chapter. We asked "What would you do if you didn't have to work any more?" Look at your answers. Did they focus on spending more money, or with spending more time with those for whom you care? Did your answer involve serving yourself or being in service to others? Did your answer focus on cash, or relationships? If relationships trumped cash, you are in good company.

Experts on human happiness and contentment have consistently found that "people with rich networks of active social relationships are much more likely to call themselves 'happy,' and are much more likely to be described as 'happy' by friends." They conclude that "true wealth is a rich network of loving people, a pleasant and healthy lifestyle, a beautiful environment, and an inviting setting for expressing creativity."[xlviii] They contrast a life of caring relationships to a life, the focus of which is money-- "a heavy burden, isolating its owner from real affection, ennobling unhealthy addictions, harming the environment, and causing boredom, frustration, and anxiety."[xlix]

Our anecdotal perspective is not different. When we ask managers who find satisfaction in their work "Why?" the most common response is, "I like the people there"— another way of saying they enjoy positive, healthy relationships with their co-workers and employees. And when we ask, "What is you dislike or resent most about your work?" the answers we most often hear are not "absence of meaningful work," or "not being paid enough money," but that "no one really cares about me," lamenting a profound, yet common, sense of loneliness in most workplaces.

It is caring relationships among people, including relationships between managers and the employees they manage, that bring satisfaction, joy, and happiness to our lives and to our work. But you don't have to take our word for it. It is a principle that has been the subject of measurement and test-retest reliability for decades. Dr. David Niven[l], for example, examined more than 1,000 happiness studies by hundreds of social scientists which have explored the characteristics and beliefs of happy people to determine what causes people to feel what we call "happiness?"[li] Researchers found:

- "Close relationships, (even) more than...one's view of the world as a whole are the most meaningful factors in happiness. If you feel close to other people, you are *four times* more likely to feel good about yourself than if you do not feel close to anyone."[lii]
- "The primary components (of happiness) are number of friends, closeness of friends, closeness of family, and relationships with co-workers and neighbors. Together, these explain about 70 percent of personal happiness."[liii]
- In surveys of employees, positive relationships with coworkers are rated as one of the most enjoyable parts of work. Sadly, that which provides us the most hope is providing most employees less satisfaction than ever before, mostly because they are looking elsewhere to find happiness and satisfaction..[liv]

Other researchers have arrived at similar conclusions by comparing how happy, content, and satisfied we feel with how close we feel to others:

- In his book *The Loss Of Happiness in Market Democracies,* Robert Lane concluded that "In prosperous countries like the United States, studies have routinely shown that the things that make people happy are family satisfaction, friendships, and relationships with other people, not money."[lv]
- Psychologist Michael Hagerty, after studying the nations with the happiest populations, found "the most important thing you can do to be happy is to develop good ties with friends and family—and you can do that wherever you are, right now."[lvi]

In another study, people who had relationships with others that allowed them to openly discuss their challenges and problems saw a 55 percent reduction in their problems over time, while those who were left on their own showed no improvement whatsoever."[lvii] Likewise, those who feel free to communicate their concerns and needs to *someone else* were 40 percent more likely to feel satisfied with their lives than those who did not."[lviii] And, it is important to note that who we have caring relationships with is relatively unimportant, researchers finding almost no differences in the happiness of those who rely on friends for companionship or those who rely upon family. "People have the capacity to experience happiness from *any* meaningful relationship and do not need all their relationships to fit the traditional model of connections with family and friends."[lix]

Such findings open a world of opportunity for every manager and supervisor in today's workplaces, each of those workplaces filled with other people with whom we spend most of our waking hours, people with whom we could create and nurture caring relationships, the source of most satisfaction in most lives.

Meaningful Human Relationships: A Functional Alternative To The Work-And-Spend Cycle

Consider these possibilities...

Could it be that we are less than satisfied at work because our expectations of what work can provide are unrealistic?

Could it be that the work and spend cycle is engineered not to make us satisfied, but to keep us busy so we never ask why we're not satisfied?

Could it be that Gary Cross was right when he suggested that "...we don't have a moral equivalent to the consumer society (such that) our notions of self-worth, of social position, of getting ahead, are all organized by consumption," and that what we desperately need is a reevaluation of how we can achieve such happiness?[lx]

Could it be that we have ignored relationships as a solution to the workplace satisfaction deficit because we have been taught to value what costs the most, and because relationships don't "cost" anything in monetary terms, we do not pursue them in the workplace?

Could it be that Robert Lane was right when he concluded, "We're not very good judges of what makes us happy. Intrinsic enjoyment of one's work has *almost* as close a relationship to happiness as does friendship."[lxi]

Could it be that the quality of our relationships at work is the key to workplace contentment and a reduction in the stress, cynicism, malaise, and loneliness that is endemic to the American workplace?

Could we introduce non-exploitive relationships into our workplaces and could those relationships be the wellsprings of personal growth, happiness and satisfaction that have heretofore eluded most of us?

Our experiences lead us to answer each question "Yes," and to conclude that caring workplace relationships, more than "more," cause each of us to appreciate our connectedness as human beings, instead of focusing solely on our economic dependencies and on our differences and disparities as competing units of labor. Indeed, we believe that the workplace will not advance beyond the lonely and unsatisfying place it has become until more managers understand, embrace, and take action upon this principle.

The good news is that an ever-growing community of managers are adopting the paradigm of relationship-based management, managing others as if their humanness was as important as their efficiency as a human resources. In these workplaces, traditional workplace relationships share temporal space with workplace relationships that are rooted in knowledge of others and personal interdependence that expresses that coalescence.

Unfortunately, these workplaces are still comparatively small in number because of external hurdles, the primary one of which is our client: corporate America.

CHAPTER 7

The "Cash Card":
Corporate America Plays Its Weakest Hand

"As a manager, my job is to sell my company's party line, like when I had to tell my employees that their new health plan with higher co-pays, deductibles, and prescription costs was "better" than the one we had before. I knew I was lying and my employees knew I was lying, too, but that's what I had to do because my company was afraid of telling employees the truth. The company believes what keeps employees happy is making our wage and benefit package look good, and it spends a lot of time trying to make less look like more. My employees aren't fooled."

- Leonce, Maintenance Supervisor

A Houston man decided to play Russian roulette with a .45-caliber semiautomatic pistol. He apparently did not realize that a semiautomatic pistol, unlike a revolver with which the game is traditionally played, automatically inserts a cartridge into the firing chamber when the gun is cocked and fires a bullet each time the trigger is pulled—100% of the time. His chance of winning the game was zero.

Corporate America reminds us of our deceased Texas gamesman. Just as he thought he knew how a pistol functioned, corporate America believes it knows what makes employees satisfied: more money or at least the appearance of more money. And so they play the "cash card," pandering to the belief in the *Myth Of More*, that desperate hope that one day more money will become enough money, and with enough money we'll live happily ever after. As indicated by the rapidly declining rates of employee satisfaction, this approach has proven about as effective as a game of Russian roulette played with a semi-automatic pistol.

Studies of the impact of more money on employee satisfaction have long indicated that if an employee's pay and benefits are "competitive" with other employees doing similar work, more money is, at best, neutral to employee contentment and happiness on the job. The additional compensation is enjoyed for a brief period and then quickly habituated, having no long-term effect on the employee's satisfaction.

But, assume for a moment that we are wrong and those who have studied what makes people happy and employees satisfied are wrong, too. Let's assume that if employees were paid more, future results would differ from past results and that employees' subjective happiness would skyrocket, and along with it, their productivity. Even if that were true, it would not solve the problem of declining employee satisfaction. Even if more money and better benefits were the answer to employee contentment, satisfaction and happiness at work, employees would still be in dire straits because there has not been "more" for the average American employee in a long time, and that reality is unlikely to change in the foreseeable future.

Wages: $300 Raise Over Ten Years

No more? Correct. The prototypical two-wage-earner family averaged $44,250 a year in 1999, just $300 more per year in inflation-adjusted wages than they earned a decade earlier.[lxii] Fast forward to 2003. During the purported rebound in the economy—a rebound that did not add jobs or put more money into employees' pockets—the average employee experienced wage and benefit increases less than inflation.

We have to go all the way back to the early 1970s to find the last time the average American employee was enjoying wage and benefit increases commensurate with his increases in productivity. The peak in average employee wages on an inflation-adjusted basis occurred more than a quarter century ago, in 1974.[lxiii] Since then, it's been down-hill for Joe Lunchbucket.[lxiv] While corporate execs enjoyed increases averaging 44% annually during the period of 1988 through 1997, Joe suffered an inflation-adjusted income drop of 11% during the same period.[lxv]

Yet "more" is the card most companies play to trump employee dissatisfaction, even though it is the weakest card in corporate America's hand. There hasn't been any more for the average employee in many years.

The Juggling Act—Making Less Look Like More

With the promise of "more," corporate America has tried to bluff its way into a winning hand by making less look like more. We know. We spent years working the numbers behind wages, producing dog and pony shows for employers that replaced defined benefit pension plans with less expensive (and less lucrative) 401k savings plans. We played the shell game of dwindling, yet increasingly expensive, health care benefits. We even explained in terms no one could understand why 3 percent was a "great raise" in pay, even though profits in the same company skyrocketed 20 percent in the same year. You have probably heard the saying, "Figures don't lie, but liars figure." It's true. Let's take a look at how it is done.

Medical Insurance: Going, Going, Soon To Be Gone

As with stagnating wages, most employees have taken it on the chin in the benefits department, too. In 1988, for example, 52% of large employers paid 100% of their employees' medical insurance premiums. Today, only 17% foot the full freight for medical insurance premiums and only 13% for their employees and dependents.[lxvi] It is why 25 percent of those working for the largest companies are now without medical insurance.[lxvii] And it is getting worse, with health insurance premiums rising 12.7 percent in 2002, the largest increase since 1990, and the reason emergency rooms have become the primary source of primary care for the working poor.[lxviii]

Even employees who do have jobs that offer medical insurance oftentimes don't really "enjoy" it, or even use it. From insurance that once paid costs for "ordinary and customary" medical services to a physician of the employee's choosing, nine out of ten employees today are faced with health care via a "network"—a euphemism for doctors bought, owned, and operated by the nation's largest insurers. Today, only 10% of employers offer indemnity medical coverage, down from 70% as recently as 1988,[lxix] leading to medical care being parceled out by corporations, not doctors, sometimes with bizarre limitations on getting any care at all. One California HMO, for example, implemented a rule that a patient can only ask two questions to the doctor per visit. That way they can maximize the number of patients a doctor can see in a single day.

Not only has the quality of medical care that is offered to most employees been reduced, but managed care hasn't met its intended purpose to hold the line on medical costs. The average monthly employee contribution for comparatively inferior health coverage has increased from $8 in 1988 to $30 in 2001 for an individual, and from $52 to $150 for family coverage over the same period.[lxx] The percentage of employees paying no co-payment for doctors' visits has been cut in half from 10 percent in 1996 to 5 percent in 2001, and if the doctor's drug of choice is not on the insurance company's "formulary," i.e., list of approved drugs, they are often not covered under managed care plans, leaving employees to pay out-of-pocket for medication they need but often cannot afford. It is not surprising that the amount Americans spend each year on prescription drugs since 1998 has increased by 40%.[lxxi]

To make matters worse, many companies pass off a majority of health care cost increases to their employees. The Institute Of Management and Administration survey of benefits professionals in 2001 found that 51.7% of employers consider "increased cost sharing by employees" as the "most successful cost-control strategy," outpacing any other strategy by more than 2 to 1.[lxxii]

Yet most employers continue to try and paint a smiley-face on managed care in a desperate attempt to make less look like more, and when it comes to premiums, more look like less. As one corporate benefits' specialist told us, "Our medical plan has been stripped cleaner than a new Porsche left on a New York City side street, and for many of our employees, what's left is barely drivable."

Can it get worse? Yes, and for many employees it has. Company-paid and company-sponsored medical insurance is disappearing altogether for millions of workers. Retiree medical insurance was once the standard for major employers; now only slightly more than half of all major employers even offer retiree medical benefits, leaving the fantasy of retirement and escape from work before age 65 just that—a fantasy.

After the hit-and-run job done on the American employee *vis a vis* health care, corporate America's contention that "your health plan is better than ever" is recognized by most employees to be what one manager summarized as "full-bore BS."

Retirement? Not Now, Not Ever

Like wages and medical care, there is no "more" in retirement, either. There is only less made to look like more. Before the popularization of the 401(k) plan, most employees knew to the penny the amount they would receive in retirement each month when they reached normal retirement age. 84% of employees of medium-to-large companies participated in traditional pension plans in 1980, which plummeted to just 52 percent by 1995. These retirement plans, more accurately called "defined benefit" plans, were so nominated because they defined the benefit to the employee, not the contribution of the employer. Under these plans, employers contributed an amount based on an actuarial calculation that determined how much needed to be set aside in order to insure the promised retirement benefits to the employee.

No large companies have formed a defined benefit pension plan in more than a decade, and many of those companies that still have defined benefit plans have juggled the numbers to reduce their contributions, resulting in what Robert J. Samuelson describes as "the pension time bomb… that could ultimately explode in a savings-and-loan-like crisis. An aging workforce and the collapse of the stock market have combined to create massive underfunding of traditional corporate pensions. The government agrees. The Pension Benefit Guaranty Corporation (PBGC), the agency that insures defined benefit pensions, estimates the underfunding at $300 billion, up from only $23 billion as recently as 1999."[lxxiii]

401(k)—"Roll Your Dice" Retirement

During the same period that pension plans were being scrapped, employees covered by 401(k) plans went from zero to a third.[lxxiv] Why? They are cheaper. With the disappearance of the defined benefit pension plan, the cost of pensions to employers declined precipitously, from 63 cents per hour of work in 1979 to 45 cents in 1996.[lxxv]

Ironically, 401(k) plans were intended by Congress to be an adjunct—that is, an addition to employer's traditional pension plans—not their replacements. Yet the 401(k) and other similar plans that fix employer contributions are ubiquitous, now sold as full-blown retirement plans. In fact, in most companies today, 401(k) savings plans are the *only* retirement plans.

Unlike the defined benefit plan, what an employee has available at retirement at the end of Highway 401(k) is the sum of what he contributed, the amount his employer has matched, plus investment results, if any. In short, the 401(k) is retirement "wheel of fortune"-style. If you spin well, make wise and/or lucky investment decisions, have an employer who liberally matches your contributions, take investment risks prudently, and the stock market cooperates, you can win the retirement jackpot. But if you do not squirrel away enough, either because you ignore your future needs, have too many bills to pay in the present, your employer reduces matching levels, or you take too much or too little risk in the stock market, you may lose big, ending up with a paltry sum, living in a single-wide trailer on the outskirts of town.

While benefits' hucksters tout the 401(k) as superior to the "old-style" defined-benefit plan,[lxxvi] research has shown that the average 401(k) participant earns 2% less a year than defined benefit plan participants, which doesn't sound like much until you consider that an employee in mid-career with $100,000 in plan assets will accumulate approximately 57% less by normal retirement age, even assuming the same level of contribution.[lxxvii] For a mid-career employee with $100,000 in 401(k) plan assets, that means $775,000 less at retirement when he walks out the door at age 65.[lxxviii] Considering that the average 401(k) plan in 1998 contained just $16,000[lxxix] *before* the stock market meltdown of 2000, the reduced results of the 401(k) only adds insult to injury.

Like medical insurance and wages, employers have sold the 401(k) hard, appealing to employees' "independence," touting "options" for investment, and the need to be "empowered," while in fact the primary purpose 401(k) was to relieve corporate America of its once assumed responsibility to make contributions to attain a target retirement benefit for its long-term employees.

As with medical insurance coverage, it can always get worse, and for many employees it has. In the recession of 2001, many major employers cut or suspended contributions to their employees' 401(k) accounts. Others tied their contribution obligations to the success of the company, leaving employees of these companies wondering if, how much, and when they could ever retire.[lxxx]

Still other employers have reduced costs by requiring employees to accept matching contributions in company stock rather than cash, such as Aetna and Proctor & Gamble. In these cases, the "no-cash 401(k)" can be the financial version of going down with a sinking ship. Employees at Lucent, for example, saw their stock lose 80 percent of its value in the year ending May, 2001. Employees at Proctor & Gamble, while doing better by investing in their company's stock, are performing a high wire act with their retirement plan since employees can own only P&G stock in their 401(k) until they reach age 50.[lxxxi]

PepsiCo promotes their 401(k) as "the most state-of-the-art plan in the market today," matching employee contributions with Pepsi stock options. If this no-cash, no value version of the 401(k) contribution is indeed "state of the art," then Pepsi employees had better feel lucky, because such a plan violates the cardinal rule that investments should be balanced and diversified, and that a single company's stock is a far riskier investment than most employees would opt for, if given the choice.

Those employers that do match employee contributions with cold, hard cash and let their employees invest 401(k) funds as they please oftentimes require the investments be made through certain mutual fund companies, most of which perpetually under-perform the market because of their fees to manage the funds. It is not surprising why so few companies do a good job educating their employees on investing and financial planning.[lxxxii] If they did, they would have to explain to their employees that their 401(k) plan violates sound investment principles.[lxxxiii]

The Cafeteria Plan: "Here's $5; Buy Yourself Childcare or Healthcare, But Not Both."

With the 401(k), corporate America effectively shifted the responsibility of providing pensions for employees to those same employees. Using the same play book and applying it to other benefits, the "cafeteria plan" entered the benefits picture stage right. Cafeteria plans are simple and straightforward; they provide employees fixed-dollar amounts from which they can shop from a varied list of benefits on a pre-tax basis, the cost and quality of which vary dramatically. Choices under these plans often include health insurance, disability coverage, child care, and accidental death and dismemberment, just to name a few. It reads like a smorgasbord of benefits, and while it appears to be a buffet, it's not. The entrees are priced *a la carte*. You can have anything you want on the menu, but only if you can afford it. The cost of child care alone exceeds the total value of cafeteria benefits offered to many employees today,[lxxxiv] leaving no money for health insurance or any other benefits.

Like managed medical care and 401(k)'s, cafeteria plans are sold by employers as "more," allowing employees to "custom-design" their benefit plans. In fact, cafeteria plans were designed to permit employers to cap their benefit costs, putting the onus on employees to select between needed benefits. Cafeteria plans also provide employers a moral defense to providing a benefit package that would leave some employees sick and penniless. "If you hadn't elected prescription coverage, Joe, you could have afforded that disability insurance, so it's not our fault that you are now disabled without any income other than what the government provides." The truth for many companies is, "We punish lower income and special-needs employees who cannot supplement company benefits that have been capped."[lxxxv]

The Meek Shall Inherit The Earth. Well, Not So Fast.

The shell game of making less look like more has been used by employers for at least 25 years, since employee productivity and employee compensation somehow got disconnected. It has been a necessary deception, since most employers are enablers of the *Myth of More,* which requires a credible claim of more to be believable. It is not that corporate America's hierarchy is made up of pathological liars. Indeed, most executives with whom we work do not lie straight-faced to their employees, but neither are most executives up to telling their employees the way it is—that the economic cuts suffered over the last quarter century have resulted not in more, but in less; that wages may match inflation but that is all for the foreseeable future;[lxxxvi] that benefits will continue to shrivel; and that employees will continue to assume more traditional benefit costs within jobs that are marginalized by the fact of their impermanence.

Most employees with whom we have spoken are not fooled by the smoke-and-mirror routine. They simply shake their heads and hope that no more of their wages or benefits will disappear between now and the time they can retire. As one mid-manager told us, tongue-in-cheek, "It appears our reward, if any, will come in heaven." Employees nod their heads in company benefits meetings and execs believe they are agreeing, when in reality they are nodding because they fear being singled out for employee execution if they object and publicly report that the king is wearing no clothes. Given an opportunity to speak freely, employees and mid-level managers are cynical, not accepting corporate America's proposition that Adam Smith's invisible hand is going to suddenly stop punching them in the face.

"Who's Got The Cheese?"

"So, where did the money go? Who's got the cheese?" asks the American employee—that difference between the increase in productivity and the increase in wages that, over the decade of the 1990s, was a staggering 40 percent?[lxxxvii] If productivity is up, why are working wages growing at their slowest rate since 1995? Why is the income gap between the richest Americans and all the rest widening?[lxxxviii] Why did pretax incomes of the top 1 percent of the U.S. earners grow 104 percent from 1977 to 1989, while the median income of all earners rise less than 7 percent?[lxxxix] What happened to the lion's share of the 90s spread between productivity and workers' wage increases? Let's take a look.

Shareholders took plenty, with the average S&P 500 stock soaring 344% during that decade,[xc] shareholders who, for the most part, do not care about wages, hours, and working conditions of the employees of the companies in which they have invested. A good example of how investors think the market feels about better wages and benefits for employees can been seen in a comparison of Costco and Wal-Mart. Even after Costco recorded a 25 percent gain in profits and a 14 percent increase in sales, shareholders drove down Costco's stock by 4 percent. In *Business Week*, Stanley Holmes and Wendy Zellner noted, "One problem for Wall Street is that Costco pays its workers much better than archrival Wal-Mart Stores, Inc.'"

Commenting on the dynamic of shareholders vs. employees, Jonathan Tasini, president of the Economic Future Group, observed "whether a company treats its workers fairly and satisfies consumers does not matter to Wall Street. Stock analysts don't reward such a feat, preferring instead that a company conform to Wall Street standards by wringing out every cent from employees' wallets."[xci] And this they have done. The war between shareholders and employees is over for the time being.

Some of the productivity dividend went back into businesses, into capital investments to grow those businesses, but even with capital reinvestment, there is still a lot of cheese missing, and employees don't have to look much beyond the executive suite to find it.

During the 1990s, executive salaries burgeoned 535%. Even after the economy fast-cooled in 2000 and millions lost their jobs to downsizing, and even as the Standards & Poors (S&P) index fell 10% (its worst showing since 1976), CEO's never felt the pain.[xcii] Fully half of the largest S&P companies paid their top executives an average of $36.5 million that year, up 62% from the year before,[xciii] and the disparity in rate of compensation growth is not slowing, even now with average CEO pay more than 441 times the average pay of the average employee, and still growing at a rate twice that of the average worker.[xciv]

Joe Lunchbucket knows who got the cheese, but he also knows he can't do anything about it. Joe may know his company's CEO is paid like a rock star, even though the CEO's job could just as easily be outsourced or offshored as his own, but he also knows that no one is going to suggest that. He also knows that his labor is a world commodity and can be given over to "temporary" employees who will work for less, or split between part-time employees who will work without benefits or even shipped offshore. Joe believes, and he has a lot of evidence in his lunch pail, that the shareholders and executives of his company will continue getting theirs, even if it means balancing the budget on the backs of those with few skills and no voice, or even if it means shipping his job to India and having him train his foreign replacement.[xcv] In short, for Joe there hasn't been and there isn't going to be any "more" for a long time.

Survivors may not believe it fair that they work for minimum wage—a wage insufficient to rent a one-bedroom apartment in any county in the United States—but few complain that their CEO's are decorating their second and third homes in Martha's Vineyard.[xcvi] As one Human Resources Director told us sardonically, "Our employees don't ask why we spill more whiskey in the corporate jet each year than it would cost to give them a raise or improve their health plan. They are too afraid of what would happen."

And, many should be afraid. Tyco International is a good example of how some employers handle dissent. Tyco was a Wall Street darling for many years, specializing in buying traditional manufacturers and hacking their workforces to bits, cutting wages and benefits, usually at the end of a pistol. In Bingham, Pennsylvania, where Tyco employees earn $5.75 to $9.55 an hour making plastic hangers and "enjoy" two 15-minute breaks per shift, a five minute "water break, no lunch, and mandatory Saturday work," Tyco proposed eliminating the "ordinary and customary" health plan and replacing it with a managed care alternative. When the employees resisted, Tyco threatened massive layoffs and even plant closure and a move overseas.[xcvii] Since most employees have seen the flight of manufacturing offshore, such threats are credible, especially when made by celebrity CEO's like Dennis Kozlowski, one of Wall Street's heroes for years, now accused of orchestrating a web of deals that looted the company (to include its employees and shareholders) of at least $600 million.

Corporate America: Coming Clean

By promising employees more—more money, more benefits—corporate American plays its weakest hand if the goal is to bring satisfaction back to the workplace. Most employees know there hasn't been more for years, there isn't more now, and there will not be more for a long time, if ever. The not-so-implicit promise to employees we often hear is, "When things get better, we'll all enjoy the fruits of our sacrifices." That is, was, and will continue to be—how can we say this gently—*The Big Lie*. There are too many other stakeholders in line for Joe Lunchbucket to reasonably expect that he'll ever get another dime above what inflation requires to keep him anywhere close to even. That may come as bad news to some taciturn executives who believe in the exploitation model of motivation, trying to make less look like more by revising history or projecting a future that is unlikely to present itself.

It is time corporate America comes clean and begins dealing from the top of the deck about money, the global marketplace, and the future. By continuing to relegate the entire workplace experience to economics, business is playing cards it doesn't have. As one Director of Labor Relations for a large company summarized his company's human relations problem to us, "We've made a big mistake. We've taken and taken and taken from our employees until there's nothing left to take. Then we lied about it."

The Hidden Suit In The Winning Hand: Relationships

If more money and benefits—or more commonly, the appearance of more money and benefits—is indeed corporate America's weakest hand, then it behooves business to find a stronger suit if the goal is to make the workplace a better place, one where employees are satisfied, if only because satisfied employees are more productive and more likely to stay around. So, what do employees really want? What do they need to feel "reasonably satisfied?"

In asking what motivates the top performers at Southwest Airlines, for example, the answer was not "pay and benefits." After all, Southwest Airlines pilots make less than their larger airline counterparts, even though they log more flight hours per day. Southwest flight attendants clean planes between flights, and many even help while they are off duty. How? Via a culture of "happiness."[xcviii] Herb Kelleher, Southwest's founder, believed that great relationships among employees led to fun and humor and hugs and were essential to a successful company. He was right. Employees of Southwest Airlines are among the most happy and contented employees among larger employers, and Southwest Airlines has been the only profitable airline among the 9 major airlines for several years.

Unfortunately, only a relative handful of large companies like Southwest Airlines have adopted a relationship-based management model, most adopting a more traditional "employee as a unit of labor" model.[xcix] It is small businesses, more often than large, that have forged new trails by focusing on and implementing relationship-based management. John Murphy, the owner of several stores within the Baskin Robbins ice cream franchise, believes meaningful personal contact between supervisors and employees on a consistent basis is the secret of employee retention. "When you show that personal interest in your employees, it empowers them to show that same interest in others. That translates to a cohesive employee team and satisfied customers." It sounds good, but does it translate to the bottom line? Yes; while the average tenure of an employee in the quick-service industry is about 90 days, Murphy has employees with tenure dating to the very beginnings of his business (8 years), with an average tenure of three years—12 times the national average for that industry.[c]

Results of studies comport with this anecdotal perspective. In *First, Break All The Rules*,[ci] Buckingham and Coffman, Gallup researchers, analyzed over 80,000 interviews with employees, and they identified those factors that result in workplaces with the highest employee "contentment"—a synonym for "satisfaction" and "happiness." They found that employee contentment and resulting workplace strength, *i.e.*, efficiency, is best measured by a dozen factors. Tellingly, many of the factors they found critical are functions of positive, personal relationships in the workplace, to include whether:

- "my supervisor, or someone at work, seems to care about me as a *person*,"
- "there is someone at work who encourages my development,"
- "at work, my opinions seem to count," and
- "I have a best friend at work."

Buckingham and Coffman found that of five factors inextricably linked to employee retention, two of them, *i.e.*, "someone cares for me as a person," and "my opinions count," are a function of positive *relationships* with others in the workplace, particularly relationships between employees and their immediate supervisors. They concluded, "It's not so much opportunities for raises or promotion through the ranks that keep employees happy. The length of an employee's stay is determined largely by his *relationship* with [his] manager."[cii] Other studies support the same conclusion. "Managers [do] trump companies," say Buckingham and Coffman, and relationships between managers and their employees trump money and traditional benefits if the goal is employee satisfaction over the long term.

As to typical methods of increasing employee satisfaction, to include institutional efforts by employers to balance work and life, (as if they were different experiences), Buckingham and Coffman concluded that whether a company has an on-site daycare facility, offers more vacation than a competitor, has a profit-sharing plan, or is committed to employee training, all "miss the mark. It's not that these employee-focused initiatives are unimportant. It's just that (the) immediate manager is more important. She defines and pervades (the) work environment. If she sets clear expectations, *knows you*, trusts you, then you can forgive the company its lack of a profit sharing program... An employee may join Disney or GE or Time Warner because she is lured by their generous benefits package and their reputation for valuing employees, but it is her relationship with her immediate manager that will determine how long she stays and how productive she is while she is there."

The evidence is overwhelming that relationship-based management works, which leads to some obvious questions:

- "Why do most employers continue juggling, promising, and trying to buy their way into employees' heads and hearts?"
- "Why have so few employers pursued relationships as an answer to the rapidly diminishing happiness of the American workforce?"

We have pondered these questions, as have Buckingham and Coffman who in an interview after publication of their book observed, "We had grown tired of not being able to convince executives that treating employees well makes them more productive. We set out to prove that if your Q12 scores go up [the answers to the 12 most significant questions related to employee satisfaction], you'll lose fewer people, face fewer worker-compensation cases, suffer less shrinkage, and earn higher profits." What they found was that employees who answered "strongly agreed" to the 12 questions were 50% less likely to turnover, 28% were more likely to work in highly productive business units, and 56% were more likely to work in units with high customer loyalty.[ciii]

Even now, several years after publication of *First, Break All The Rules* and years after other research, surveys, and a myriad of anecdotes concluded that positive human relationships are the almost important factor in employee satisfaction, there has not been a mass movement toward relationship-based management.

Why? Because there are more hurdles that have not been leapt...

CHAPTER 8

Relationships: Hurdles For The Overworked, Overinformationed, Conflicted Manager

I can give you a lot of fancy words for a simple idea. It is people, and people alone, that make this place work. They may only stack stuff, but they are people nonetheless. I began here stacking. If you take the time to know them, their families, their lives, to help them with their problems and share their joys and sorrows, they will follow you anywhere. But if you cannot find the time to listen, or if you ever get so high up the ladder that you do not hear those at the bottom, then you will not be successful. What companies need to hear is this: "Our employees are here the same as you are here, and probably for the same reason. They bleed, they hurt, and they feel, too. They want you to feel what they feel. To do that, you must know them—not as workers, but as people."

- Jim, first-line manufacturing manager

MOST managers with whom we work feel like Jim, even though they may not express it with such passion. They feel empathy toward their employees. They regularly help their employees with personal problems. They know, or at least intuit, that relationships are an important and rewarding aspect of their job, both to them and to their employees, and they are correct.

The National Opinion Research Center found that "people who could name five or more friends with whom they could discuss matters of personal importance were 60 percent more likely to feel 'very happy' than others who could list none."[civ] Can you list five friends in your workplace? Would each of your employees list you among five friends in their workplace? Would each of your employees conclude that you know enough about them to really understand who they are and what they feel?

If not, why not?

Most managers respond, "Because I don't have the time to know everyone I manage at that level." Still other managers regurgitate the age-old adage, "You shouldn't get too close to your employees," and obey the directive without examination. And a handful of managers fail to see any value in personal workplace relationships, usually because they have never experienced one.

Regardless of reason, most managers know less about their own employees after working with them for two years than they know about a movie character after sitting in a theatre for two hours. When we ask managers to "write down the names of each of your employees and the names of their spouses and each of their children," most just sit and struggle to remember a few names. Yet when we ask them to write down the name of their three favorite TV characters and the names of their spouses and children, they do so with ease. They spend far more time with their employees than they spend with their TV friends. Why don't they know more?

The Overworked Managers: "We're Just Too Busy!"

Most managers plead "no time" to really get to know their employees. They have a facially-valid defense. With the leaning of the ranks of mid-management since the 1980s, most managers supervise more employees, giving each manager less time to know each employee and to experience the empathy required to establish meaningful relationships.

"I'd love to know my employees better, but take a look at this!" one manager exclaimed, pointing alternatively to a precarious mound of paper on his desk and an ever-changing spreadsheet on his computer monitor. Like most managers, he is overworked. American managers put in the longest hours in the industrialized world, logging more hours on the job than either their Japanese or Korean counterparts, both vaunted workaholics. With laptops, cell phones, beepers, home fax machines, and other technological paraphernalia, managers are virtually tethered to their offices. "I automate tasks, preview my messages, never handle any piece of paper more than once, and take care not to duplicate my efforts, but I'm still falling farther behind," one manager summed up her unsuccessful efforts to deal with the time pressures brought on by overwork.[cv]

As another manager explained, "We are working as hard as we can; there are no more hours in a day which we can spend working."[cvi] That is true for many managers and non-managers alike. The International Labor Organization estimates that the average American works 1,978 hours each year, 350 hours—nine weeks—more than Western Europeans. The average American actually worked 199 hours more in 2000 than he did in 1973, a period during which worker productivity per hour nearly doubled.[cvii]

Corporate America has heaped even more work on its managers, giving them little time and less encouragement for what many companies view as "optional" activities, including a commitment to building relationships inside the workplace. Thus, in most companies, any method devised to create meaningful relationships between managers and those they supervise must take up little, if any, additional management time.

The Cynics: "If Employees Want Their Mama, They Won't Find Her Here."

Some purported management experts object contending any effort by employers to be "more than a paycheck" to their employees is futile. It is not that corporate America is failing to meet employees' needs, the corporate apologists argue, but rather that employees have too many needs to be met. Dave Arnott in *Corporate Cults: The Insidious Lure Of The All-*

Consuming Organization opines that "job satisfaction has been declining for years because employees are expecting the wrong things from the workplace...they are expecting emotional satisfaction from work, not just financial satisfaction." Others second this motion, like Benjamin Hunnicutt who opines:

> *It's a myth that we can find identity, meaning, and community at work. I call it the Mary Tyler Moore myth. Everyone thinks they will go to work and find a wonderful group of people to serve as family and friends, like Mary Tyler Moore did in the 1970s sitcom. In reality, employees find dullards and irrational bosses. The idea that employees can find community and people to love in a highly political environment like the workplace is flawed, because work is about control.*[cviii]

Interesting, but we have not yet heard an actual line manager—as opposed to putative experts—make that argument, and there is a reason they don't make that argument. That argument is wrong, even dangerous, giving corporate America dispensation from encouraging the very condition that can bring satisfaction and happiness into their workplaces. These nihilistic perspectives, if true, would destine employees to continue the downward spiral into ever greater workplace dissatisfaction and unhappiness, or transmogrify them into emotionless automatons 8 or 10 hours a day. We have seen many workplaces filled with managers who meet employees' needs for more than a paycheck, and do so successfully and profitably.

The Conflicted Manager: "Don't Get Too Close To Your Employees!"

A few managers justify their lack of knowledge about, interest in, empathy for, and resulting relationships with employees by clinging to the age-old admonition, "You shouldn't get too close to your employees." During a session in New York City, we happened upon a manager who had supervised an employee for more than thirty years and yet did not know his last name, whether he was married, or if he had any children. Far more shocking was the fact he was not the least bit embarrassed by his ignorance, snorting, "What good is all that information to me?" The fact that this manager was rated "worst" among all managers on an employee survey was not surprising, nor was his bitterness with work and his explicit desire to "retire and get the hell out of here!" His banal misanthropy and permanent scowl, combined with the soul-dead masks worn by his employees, were dead giveaways.

The atavistic prohibition against personal relationships in the workplace assumes that too much knowledge is a dangerous thing. If that were true, a good argument could be made for not knowing too much about your children for fear of "getting too close" and affecting your decisions. Employees, much like children to their parents, look to their managers for direction, guidance, discipline, as well as for care, acceptance, and recognition. In short, we have seen no evidence that the ability of a manager to supervise is damaged or marginalized by knowing his employees, empathizing with them, caring for them as human beings, and enjoying relationships with them. In fact, many first-line managers know this intuitively and genuinely resent any attempt by their employers to roadblock relationships[cix]— healthy, caring relationships that bring happiness and satisfaction to work.[cx]

Most modern managers agree that knowing their employees—really knowing them as human beings, as opposed to human resources—is important, even essential to being an effective manager. In our training sessions, most managers nod their heads in unison when we discuss their roles as "mothers, fathers, brothers, sisters, pastors, mentors, teachers, and psychiatrists." More importantly, most managers assume these roles and take them seriously, trying to wear the right hats on the right days with the right employees, yet they admit they often fail playing these roles consistently or well.

Pleading "I don't have time" or being torn by "conflicting demands," managers complain that when push comes to shove and the product has to get out the door, the cause of relationships goes out the window, replaced with impersonality, insensitivity, and brute force. One supervisor summarized the problem of developing workplace relationships like this: "We're told, even trained, to get to know our employees and be sensitive to their needs, but, no one here really believes that is important, at least not to the company. After all, we're not evaluated on the relationships we've built with our employees. When one of my employees needed time away from work to watch her child's first play at school, I went to my manager who told me, 'If you can accommodate him, do it, but only if you can get the production out the door.' I understood that to mean, 'To hell with your employee; the customer comes first.'" The COO of the same company told us with unexamined self-assurance, "It's not that our managers' 'soft skills' are unimportant. It's just they're not *as* important as our customer's needs, desires, and whims." After all, the customer is always right," he smiled as if he was the first one to coin that phrase.

With "the customer comes first" as the prevailing attitude in corporate America, it is not surprising that managers are conflicted, understanding on a personal level the importance of knowing their employees, but simultaneously being infused with the nonsensical contention that "the customer is *always* right," even when it is obvious that customers are often wrong, demanding, and sometimes irrational. Relationship-based managers in such environments admittedly have it tough, on the one hand feeling compassion for their employees, yet knowing on the other that when the customer pulls the string, their mouth has to move.

The "Overinformationed" Manager: "I Can't Put One More Fact Into My Head!"

Along with being overworked and conflicted, there is still another hurdle for managers wishing to create and nurture meaningful relationships in the work place: information overload. The amount of information the average manager must know, remember, and manipulate, has never been greater, and it is growing every year. R. S. Wurman observed in *Information Anxiety* that "a weekday edition of *The New York Times* contains more information than the average person was likely to come across in a lifetime in 17th-century England."[cxi] There are ten thousand newspapers and magazines published in the United States, along with more than 100,000 new book titles published every year. All of that, along with 60 billion pieces of advertising junk mail and a "paperless office" that never happened, you'd think we would be buried in pulp—and we are. But paper is just a small part of our problem of being "overinformationed." The silicon chip "has amplified the instream of information until matters have reached such proportions that for the average person today, information no longer has any relation to the solution of problems."[cxii]

Managers know it. In a recent survey, one out of four managers said they have suffered ill health as a result of the amount of information they are required to know and handle. 48 percent of managers predicted that the Internet would play a primary role in aggravating the problem; 49 percent feel they are often unable to handle the volume of information they receive, and almost two-thirds of the managers say their personal relationships suffer as a direct result of information overload.[cxiii]

Managers complain relentlessly about having "too many balloons in the air" and express fear that "one of those balloons will touch the ground because I can't remember what I need to remember. There is just too much!" For these managers, the workplace is a force-fed information dumping ground that has translated their lives into confusion, frustration, and a lack of focus. They are victims of mental ataxia, brought on by too many demands, fed by too much information and exacerbated by too little assistance, a dearth of recognition, with not even a bone being thrown to their humanity. One manager summed it up this way: "I feel like one of those geese they force-feed by nailing their feet to the floor and pushing food into them until they literally explode. There is just no more room in my head. How can I learn enough about each of my employees to have real relationships with them?" For these confounded souls, any new information, program, or "roll-out" is met with deep sighs, cynical smirks, or beseeching glances toward the heavens. Too much information, like too much work, is a common reason managers plead "no time" to pursue relationships in the workplace, and one that must be respected in any viable solution.

Overwork, Conflicted, and Overinformationed: Objections Overruled

The hurdles to workplace relationships for most managers—overwork, conflict, and information overload—are real. Managers, expected to accomplish too much in too little time, are real. Managers who supervise too many employees are real.[cxiv] Too much information is also real, all leading to the question, "Combined with ever-increasing demands on a manager's time, can there be time for anything else?" In other words, regardless of their importance, is there time for managers to build non-traditional relationships with employees when there are so many widgets to assemble, programs to write, and customers to service? One manager succinctly expressed his dilemma, "I have 32 employees and I'd like to know them all, because they'd be happier and so would I, but I don't have time to go to the bathroom. So how do I make time? About now, you may be wondering the same thing.

The answer is that you have time to build relationships with each of your employees if you can spare, find, beg, cajole, or borrow 15 minutes a day from another task— personal or professional.

The modern manager's challenge is to find that 15 minutes in each day and set it aside to develop, remember, and utilize important information necessary to create meaningful relationships. This is where the Credible Connections relationship-building tools come into play: *Milestone Cards*, the *Manager's Journal*, and *Care Cards*. They will insure that you know, remember, and acknowledge important events, people, and dynamics in your employees' lives, which will naturally and inevitably result in empathy and the formation of the relationships that lead to workplace satisfaction.

PART IV

The Relationship-Based Manager's Toolbox

CHAPTER 9

The Milestone Box: Knowing and Remembering

I never believed that simply remembering some basic facts about my employees' lives would cause me to feel differently about them, but the Milestone Box has done just that. As I think about it, all my meaningful relationships—inside and outside the workplace— have as their foundation what I know about others. We in the HR department have used the three tools alongside our line managers, and our ability to serve employees has been increased by a factor of magnitude.

- Bill, HR Director

WE cannot share relationships with people we do not know, and we cannot know others without knowing important things about them. It is the failure to know important facts about, and events in, the lives of our employees that limits managers' ability to create and nurture meaningful relationships.

This need for overworked managers to remember important facts and events in employees' lives led to the development of the first of our three relationship-building tools. The *Milestone Box* is a simple, low-tech, but highly effective, tool of recording significant events in the lives of employees that allows managers to summon up these events for future reference, understanding, and communication, the combination of which leads naturally to the formation of relationships.

The Milestone Box—Circa 1978

The Milestone Box has an interesting genesis, developed in 1978 by a young man who had taken over from his father as the president of a soft-drink bottling company. Hank had been at the helm less than a year when he was summoned to a meeting in the company's auditorium. There he found three hundred angry employees shouting about everything from wages to hours, working conditions to supervisory mistreatment and neglect. He was shell-shocked, not so much by the nature of the complaints, but by what he described as "my ignorance of the people. I looked out into that audience," he recalled, "and other than my management team, I could not have told you the names of ten of those people. I came out of college a 'numbers-man,' and had always believed that my father wasted a lot of time getting to know every employee, but his wisdom became very clear to me that morning. I decided I was going to know each of my employees. The nagging question I faced was, 'How?'"

Hank knew the way to get to know someone was to learn something about them, preferably something important. He began by listing important events in his own life, believing that the same events were important to others, too. Once his list was complete, he set out to know each employee by learning something important about them.

When he arrived at the plant each morning, rather than sitting down and pouring over spreadsheets, Hank spent the first fifteen minutes of each day walking around the plant and talking to employees. He used employee birthdays and dates-of-hire he had pulled from personnel files as a reason to introduce himself. He found that this broke the ice, and he began conversations that led to learning of other important events in his employees' lives. He would then return to his office and write down anything significant he had learned.

It was not long before the scraps of paper were piling up, and Hank knew that they would soon become useless to him unless they were organized and filed in a way that he could access them when he needed them. That morning he asked his secretary to buy him some index cards, dividers, and a box to put them in.

Hank first considered creating one card on each employee, listing the important events on each card, and alphabetizing the cards by last name, but he realized that this would require him to review every card in his box on a daily basis. He didn't have that kind of time.

He next considered having a card for each important event, to include employee birthdays, anniversary dates, deaths in the family, and awards, but, he realized that if, for example, all employee birthdays were written on one card, he would have to review the card on which all birthdays were written in order to determine whether that day was an employee's birthday.

This left one other variable by which to organize the significant events in his employees' lives: the date of the event. *"That's it!"* Hank thought. Not by employee, not by the type of event, but by the date of the event which he wanted to remember, follow up, discuss, communicate, or acknowledge. Even better, he thought, he could take each index card and note on the top of the card the date on which he wanted to follow up on that event and then write a brief description of the event itself. In the case of birthdays and anniversaries, he would file them in his card box to follow up yearly. In the case of an employee returning from hospitalization, he could schedule a follow-up a day, week, or month in advance.

It worked. For the next twenty-five years, Hank never sat down in his chair until he had, in his words, "done my cards," which to him meant pulling the cards out of the box for that day and approaching employees for whom that date had significance, and then recounting and acknowledging their milestone events with them.

Over the years, Hank's card box grew, and by the time he retired twenty-five years later, he knew the names of every employee, their birthdays, the names of their children, challenges they had faced, and a myriad of other important facts about each of them. That he had these facts available in his card box regularly reminded him to share a minute or two of his time with others to let them know that he, the boss, knew something about them, something important.

From three hundred angry employees he didn't know to becoming a revered manager, Hank's card box was a success. But of course it was not the card box. Rather, it was Hank's care, compassion, and concern that the card box allowed him to show to each employee. That made all the difference. The card box was the vehicle Hank used to sort, recall, and use all that information in the creation of relationships.

Since then, thousands of managers have followed in Hank's tracks, setting up *Milestone Boxes*. The next manager to set up a *Milestone Box* will be you, and the steps are simple and straight-forward:

Step One: Identify Milestones

Your first step is to decide what it is you should know and remember about your employees. The easiest way to do that is to look within. What significant events have occurred in your life—events you appreciated being acknowledged by others? Before continuing, write them down.

Now, add those to these events that we and other managers have come up with. We have divided life's most important events into two categories: (1) *Significant Emotional Events* and (2) *Milestone Events*. Review each event in these two categories and add them to your list if they are not already there.

Significant Emotional Events

The most important events in any life are "significant emotional events"—events that touch us most deeply, mark us indelibly, and change the way we think about the world and about others. We remember significant emotional events for the rest of our lives without a conscious effort to so.

If you have ever lost a parent, a spouse, or a close friend to death, you probably remember what you were doing at the moment you learned of their death, even if it occurred 20 years ago. The event was so significant to you that it marked your brain's directory track forever. It is true for you and for everyone who has lost a close loved one. Because we experience the same, or similar, significant emotional events, we can empathize with others who have experienced similar events. The irony is that even though we recognize certain events to be significant in others' lives because the same, or similar, events have been significant in our own lives, we do not often remember the events in their lives except as they affect us or those with whom we have close relationships.

What are these significant emotional events? Psychologists tell us that the following events are the most important in our lives—events we will always remember, and the events that are remembered by people with whom we have the closest relationships:[cxv]

- *Marriage*

Love takes most of us to the altar, and if you are in love or ever have been in love, you know that love transcends all other emotions. Marriage is the celebration of love for the most significant other in our life and ideally begins a lifelong relationship, one of unconditional care, compassion, and concern, reciprocal in every way— consoling, sharing, and intimate.

The event of marriage is both a joyous and reverent time, and significantly one of the few ceremonies— purificatory and propitiatory—that remains in Western culture. Thus it is not surprising that those with whom we share meaningful relationships remember and acknowledge the anniversary of our marriage. Every manager should do the same for those with whom he wishes to share meaningful relationships.

- *Birth*

Asked to "describe the most memorable moments in your life," most managers with children answer without hesitation, "The days my children were born." While not celebrated with a formal ceremony like marriage, the birth of a child is both the creation of life and the assumption of a lifelong obligation. We never forget our children's birthdays, and neither do our employees forget their children's birthdays. Remembering our employees' birthdays and the birthdays of their children allows us to become a part of important moments in their lives every year.

- *Death of a Loved One*

This final step in every life—the only step we can count upon absolutely—is death. Ironically, it is the one event few of us plan for, except for our beloved stuff which we take great care to parcel out in wills and trusts. Prepared or not, the shock and angst that results from the death of a loved one is also often a wake-up call for those given an up-close view of mortality.[cxvi]

What has been the traditional corporate response to this significant emotional event in the lives of their employees? "Grieve; just don't take too long." From ridiculous policies that permit "three days off" for "death of a spouse," to overworked managers who put humanity aside in order to solve their current production needs, most companies and managers have done a poor job of helping employees handle death, and very few have used death as an opportunity to create meaningful relationships through the expression of care, compassion, and concern.

When an employee suffers a death in her immediate family, the manager needs to express not only compassion, but understanding,[cxvii] and to understand, the manager must remember. Over the weeks and months that follow the death of someone significant to an employee, the caring manager shows compassion because he remembers.

As you learn of significant emotional events in your employees' lives write them into your *Milestone Box*. Know that you need not pry into the personal lives of your employees, but simply listen and record them. Employees commonly share joys, sorrows, epiphanies, and awakenings with their managers, and more often with managers who listen, understand, remember, and recall. Most employees want to prove to others, and even to themselves, that their lives have meaning beyond financial utility. It is the baring of our souls via communication of life-changing experiences that presents human vulnerability that, if understood and remembered, are the foundation of meaningful relationships that bring satisfaction and happiness to the giver and the recipient.

Milestone Events

Not all important events in our lives are as acute or emotionally intense as the birth of a child or death of a loved one. What other events made your list? As you are reviewing your list, consider the events that did not make your list: "failed to make my numbers," "received no bonus three years ago," and "terrible customer satisfaction survey." Interesting, isn't it?

Now, take your list and divide the remaining events into those you deem "pleasant" and those you deem "painful."

Now, let's compare the rest of your list with the compendium of events managers list most often.

Milestone Events (Pleasant)

As you add to your list of milestone events, ask yourself, "How effective would I be if I could remember each of these events in every one of my employees' lives?"

- *Acts of kindness*

Most of us tend to remember acts of compassion and generosity, whether it is an act of great magnanimity like saving a life or an act as simple as someone helping you change a flat tire. Indeed, one manager recalled that the genesis of a life-long relationship with an employee was a flat tire. "I never really liked Joe," his manager admitted, "but I saw him after work one afternoon on the side of the road with a flat tire and I pulled over and helped him change it. I don't know what happened that day, but in those fifteen minutes we learned more about each other than we had in the five years before. More than a tire got changed that day. We both got changed, and we became friends, and we remain friends to this day." Not a remarkable account until we spoke with Joe, who recalled the event in equally vivid detail, ascribing the same importance to this seemingly insignificant act of kindness.

- *Birthdays*

The most regularly celebrated day in most lives is the birthday. It marks temporally each person's place on earth. For some, their birthday is a time to reflect on wisdom and experience gained in the prior year. For others, their birthday allows the past to be packaged and put away and a new year to be unwrapped and anticipated.[cxviii]

- *Anniversaries*

In western society, we have a heritage of celebrating anniversaries of significant events. Whether it was the day your child was born, the day your little girl got married, or the day she became a parent, important events in your life are acknowledged and celebrated annually by those who care for you.

- *Significant Accomplishments*

Individual accomplishments in community service, charitable efforts, as well as work-related accomplishments in sales, service, quality, support, are sources of pride for many employees. The caring manager gives each of her employees their "15 minutes of fame," often critical to self-esteem and always helpful to relationship development.

Likewise, significant events and accomplishments by a member of an employee's family may be milestones in their lives, events like the homerun your employee's son hit in the local Little League World Series or the medical degree your employee's daughter achieved after years of formal education. How effective would it be if you could remember not only employee accomplishments, but the accomplishments of their loved ones?

- *Holidays*

The impact of holidays varies significantly by individual, belief, religion, and heritage. The alert manager learns the holidays of special import to each employee and remembers to celebrate important holidays along with them.

The list of pleasant milestone events in life goes on. Personal growth, life transitions, life simplification, philosophical epiphanies, and achievements are but a few more milestone events that provide opportunity for the relationship-based manager to remember, follow-up, empathize, and communicate with a view to creating relationships. What other pleasant milestone events made your list?

Milestone Events (Painful)

Significant life events are not always pleasant. Painful or stressful events are equally significant to our development and understanding. Studies have shown that the most common psychological and social stressors in adult life include the breakup of intimate relationships, death of a family member or friend, economic hardships, racism and discrimination, poor physical health, and accidental and intentional assaults on personal safety.[cxix]

A good example of unpleasant milestone events and how they can be used to create relationships involved an employee we'll call Barbara. She was kicked out of her house by her parents at age 17, pregnant by age 19, had her first child at age 22, and married at age 25. She decided more than once to leave her abusive husband, but the night she garnered the courage to try, she was confronted at the door with a pistol and a clear instruction to "never do that again." A week later, she discovered she was pregnant. She gave birth to a little girl—a special child, a child with Down's syndrome.

Barbara's husband, who had been married previously, brought his 9-year-old son by a prior marriage into the family, a child who had lived in more than 50 different apartments with nearly as many "daddies." Barbara caught the 9-year-old sexually abusing her son twice, but her insistence that he get help went unheeded. In the end, Barbara's husband was not up for the strain—a child in and out of the hospital gasping for breath, another wholly uncontrollable, and he walked out, leaving Barbara—now 31—with two chronically ill children, a tiny apartment in a poor neighborhood—an apartment on which the rent had not been paid, a petition for divorce, a $600-a-month child care obligation, and a job as a temporary with a big corporation that paid $12 an hour.

WHY WORK ISN'T WORKING ANYMORE

Barbara was a member of the group you will recall us discussing in Chapter 2, "the working poor." Because of a couple of unscheduled doctor visits, Barbara had no money, as in *none*. Her rent check bounced and her landlord had been to her door twice with a not-so-subtle suggestion that she needed to come up with the rent or move. But Barbara had no where to go, no one to turn to, so she dropped her children off at daycare and went to work, where she often cried silently in her cubicle wondering what would happen next.

Barbara went to her employer, who provided the traditional Employee Assistance Program which gave Barbara three sessions of "counseling." Her manager was of no help, either, writing it off to Barbara's "bad luck." Barbara was on food stamps, worked all the overtime she could get, and went without lunch so her children could eat. The bank closed her account because it had reached the overdrawn limit. She faced a court hearing for a traffic citation because she had no money for car insurance.

At Barbara's darkest moment, she was befriended by a co-worker, Kandace, a young lady just 21 years old who listened, understood, and communicated her desire to help. She spent time on the phone with various human resources personnel and social agencies, and found that neither her employer, nor the government, had any help for Barbara. It seems the new tough federal policies put into place to keep the welfare abusers off the dole have let many legitimately needy fall through the net, too.

Kandace told us, "I thought about Barbara that night as I watched a news story about huge tax breaks and subsidies given by government to the rich. I looked at our corporate EAP, which was a joke, and I looked at our manager who didn't give a damn.

"I saw all of this, and I was angered and ashamed. I understand that my company is in business to make a dollar, but this company is made up of people," Kandace told us forcefully. "So I figured if my government, my company, and manager wouldn't help, then we—Barbara's fellow employees—would help her. I went out, told Barbara's story, and asked for help. I was amazed at how many of my fellow employees stepped up to the plate, how many had themselves experienced need in their lives.

"Barbara wouldn't take money," Kandace continued. She was too proud. But because I knew her, I knew that Ellie (her daughter) and Bobby (her son) needed winter clothes and coats. The clothes and gift cards poured in. When I asked Barbara what she needed for herself, she told me, 'Nothing, I'm OK,' but I new that wasn't true. I knew she could use some white cotton panties. I know because she always joked that hers were falling apart. Barbara and I developed a relationship during all of this, and I can't help wondering how much my company and my manager missed by standing aside."

We don't wonder. The company missed an opportunity to help one of their own, to earn the loyalty they said they wanted. The manager missed the opportunity to create a relationship.

As managers, what are the events we should record? We don't have to guess. A report on mental health by the Surgeon General[cxx] reveals that the most common psychological and social "stressors," i.e., painful events, in an adult life are these:

- *Divorce*

Nearly one-half of all marriages in the United States end in divorce. 30 to 40 percent of those recently divorced report significant increases in symptoms of depression and anxiety.[cxxi] When confronted with divorce from the person to whom you once committed your life, it often seems as though your whole life—not just your marriage—is falling into the abyss, and this is especially true if you are not the one who chooses to end the relationship. The unknown future—one that is different, frightening and lonely—looms ahead. "Pain" is the first word that comes to the lips of those who have experienced a permanent separation from the one they love or once loved. A primal human fear, the fear of being alone forever, often follows.

Whether it is the personal pain from the destruction of an intimate long-term relationship or that angst felt vicariously for the children of a failed marriage, divorce remains one of the scourges of modern society and for those who experience it. Many who are divorced feel alienated from their friends, and it is in this toughest and most vulnerable of times that those managers who care also remember, and offer support.

- *Failure of intimate romantic relationships*

A variation on the theme of divorce is the end to an intimate relationship, especially one for which one or both parties had aspirations of permanency. Separation is particularly difficult when the person leaving was a source of stability to the other. Some people compare the devastation of separation with the sensation of falling and a concomitant fear that stability in their lives is gone forever.

With five percent of adult Americans now living together unmarried, up from just three percent in 1990, there are more non-marital separations than ever before, and it is not surprising that these breakups often resemble divorce and its aftermath[cxxii]. Like divorce, they lend themselves to a heightened vulnerability to depression stemming from the belief, however wrong, that they will never recover and forever be alone. In these times, we forget that we will habituate, but we often get through the process faster if there is someone who cares and shows it, someone like a caring manager.

- *Economic hardships*

You may recall from Chapter 2 that 30 percent of the U.S. population is "working poor." 35 million people go to work everyday and still cannot afford a one-bedroom apartment in any county in the United States.[cxxiii] There are hundreds of thousands of full-time employees like Barbara who work for companies of all sizes, yet who are eligible for and subsist on food stamps.

Poverty among plenty, particularly poverty that cannot be written off for "being too lazy to work," has become an embarrassment to our society, and likewise, should be an embarrassment to companies that do not pay a living wage. Regrettably, it has not become enough of an embarrassment for most companies in the service and retail industries to do anything about it. There appears to be no groundswell movement toward strengthening the social net or to significantly boost the minimum wage, and so it is not surprising that many employees find themselves working and homeless, or one paycheck away from living on the street.[cxxiv]

Society, not individual managers, will have to deal with an economy that is becoming ever more disparate. Until that happens, however, it will be left to caring individuals like Kandace, who acknowledge, follow up, and do the best they can to help with the economic hardships being experienced by their employees and co-workers.

- *Poor physical health, acute or chronic illness*

As significant as any physical challenge, illness affects us emotionally, as does the illness of others for whom we care. Managers are often caught between the need to get the job done and their empathy for sick or injured employees. From feeling sad for an afflicted employee to feeling guilty for being healthy to feeling anger because the illness of the employee affects the workload of other employees, managers can feel a panoply of emotions, the most important one of which is empathy, knowing that serious illness changes lives. Such illnesses in an employee's family often consume the caregiver, and the relationship-based manager remembers, understands, and acts accordingly.

- *Crime/Violence*

When an employee or a family member has been victimized by crime, the employee may feel anger, guilt, shame, insecurity, fear, powerlessness, or depression. Most employees find little help from their employers, and often compartmentalize these events and suffer alone until they can get home to their "real lives," where family members assist them through the emotional mending and oftentimes difficult legal process.[cxxv]
The failure of a manager to recall traumatic events in their employees' lives, some of which can lead to unacceptable and unproductive workplace behavior, too often results in unnecessary and damaging heavy-handedness, instead of support. Managers can assist the healing process by opening themselves up to hearing, learning, and understanding what their employee has suffered, treating the employee with sensitivity, recognizing that healing can be facilitated by letting the employee tell his story again and again and by working with the employee to build a network of support to include the manager, co-employees, family members, and professional counselors.[cxxvi] Through understanding, managers will not set unrealistic expectations and timetables.

- *Fear/Anxiety*

"No Fear" t-shirts and executive chest-pounding autobiographies aside, we all experience fear. Life is, after all, a journey about which we understand little, and most of us fear at one time or another that we are not living our lives to their full potential. For others, it is the fear that when life ends, it is over. Fade to black.
Regardless of fear's focus, whether it is the fear of death, disease, failure, or one of the many other loathsome events life may serve up to us, most fears are not in response to what is actually happening. Rather, most fears are fears over an uncertain future, fears that are exacerbated by our inability to accept the vagaries and uncertainties of life. "I'm afraid I *might* lose my job." How many times have you heard that? How many times have you thought it? How many of us have feared losing our jobs when we have had a bad day at work, put 2 and 2 together and have come up with 5?

How many of us have spent precious present moments fearing events that have not occurred, but that *might* occur in the future? How many of our fears are in response to a present threat, like the fear that enables a mother to do whatever she must to protect the young lives of her children when they are in danger, as opposed to fears about events we cannot control and which may never happen, and without question, are not happening now? For many people, fear of the future debilitates them, and this fear becomes an unfortunate and unwelcome milestone event in their lives.

Because fear and satisfaction are mutually exclusive, to improve the quality of life of others we must perceive, understand, remember and distinguish fear in the present from fear of the future. The best managers are those who not only live in the present, but also have the ability to draw others into the present, away from some future moment that cannot be lived, not in the now. To do this, the manager must listen to the employee's fears, understand them, empathize, and offer help.

Manager "As" Psychologist or Manager "Is" Psychologist?

A criticism sometimes leveled at our program is, "You can't make managers into shrinks." We agree; we can't. We cannot make managers into something they already are. And every manager, especially first-line managers, are *de facto* psychologists, not by title or credentials, but almost every manager with whom we have worked acknowledges that listening to employee problems—personal and professional—and helping them deal with those problems, is a significant part of their job. Teaching employees how to look at and deal with problems effectively, both inside and outside the workplace, is a task managers face on a daily basis, like it or not. The answer is not to take away what is inherently a part of their duty, but rather to make them better custodians of that duty.

That said, not all employee milestones can be handled by managers. Some situations present challenges that require professional help. Two examples come to mind immediately: clinical depression and domestic violence. Most often, these situations require professional intervention, yet few employers train their managers to even recognize them.[cxxxvii]

Perhaps your life has provided special and unique joys or challenges that go well beyond the list we have provided that will allow you to remember and exhibit compassion and concern in situations few others could handle. Perhaps you saved a life. Perhaps you saved a relationship. Maybe your life has been filled with hardship and challenges that you have not always understood, but which you overcame, events that have made you stronger, wiser, or more resilient. Perhaps you have lost a loved one and still love the one you lost, but have faced the pain and conquered it. Perhaps you learned something about life through death. Perhaps you have unresolved pain, guilt, or fear, and understand that milestone events are not only about the past, but are very much about the present and the future.

Take some time right now and update your list of milestone events. As each of your employees or co-workers is unique, so are you. Use your life of significant emotional events and milestone events and expand from where you left off, using your lists only as starting points.

Update your list of milestone events before moving to Step 2. You will use this list as a reminder as you begin logging the milestone events in your employees' lives.

Step Two: Get a Card Box, Monthly Index Tabs, 1-30 Day Tabs, and Index Cards

After your milestone list is complete, purchase some index cards, measuring three inches by four inches, and one set of index card tabs. You want the tabs labeled with the months of the year: January through December. Finally, buy one set of tabbed index cards marked 1-31, each representing a day of the month.

Those are the physical tools you'll need to implement this easy and useful tool. Like Hank, you will keep your *Milestone Box* safe and accessible so it will be available to you every day.

Step Three: Insert Tabs

Take the two sets of tabs—one set composed of twelve tabs marked January through December, and the other set containing 31 tabs marked 1 through 31—and insert both sets of tabs into the box, along with the index cards.

Using The Milestone Box

If you are looking for the hook in all of this, here it is: If you dutifully purchase the correct supplies, set up your *Milestone Box,* and then let it sit untouched on your desk, it will prove to be another waste of space. We know this because when we return for follow-up sessions, we always ask managers to bring along their *Milestone Boxes* and share with us the unique events in employees' lives they have documented and how they have used those events in service to their employees. Depending on commitment to the program and the value assigned to it in the scheme of multifarious and often conflicting corporate goals and objectives, we find differing levels of manager acceptance and success.

Using Your Milestone Card Box Daily: 5 Steps To Relationships

Where you fit into the palette of managers who have been trained to use the *Milestone Box* depends solely on you—whether you use it, how you use it, how often you use it. Like setting up your *Milestone Box,* using it is not an art form, but it does require commitment, a small leap of faith, and following these few simple steps:

Step One: Review Your Employees' Personnel Files

We advise companies who adopt the system to provide every manager two *Milestone Cards* on each of their employees: birth date and hire date. This acts as a "jump- start" for most managers. The information is generally available in the personnel file on each employee, and oftentimes there is a gold mine of other milestone events to be found there, including dates of work-related achievements, children's and spouses' birthdays, dates of marriage, and more. There is no reason to reinvent the wheel or mine for ore that has already been brought to the surface.

Step Two: Listen and Talk (In That Order)

The most common question asked about documenting employee milestones is, "How do I get my employees to share their milestones with me?" The answer is, "You don't." All you need to do is *listen*. Some employees are more circumspect than others, but when it becomes apparent that you are genuinely interested in your employees as human beings and not solely as human resources, even employees who play their cards close to the vest will begin sharing. When they do share important life anecdotes, you must listen, express interest, acknowledge and discuss the events which they share with you. Sometime during the conversation you may ask, "When did this happen?" Remember, you need the date of the event in order to complete a *Milestone Card*.

Here's an example. One of your employees, John Gallagher, comes to work one day, beaming with pride. "My wife had a baby last night!" he announces proudly to you, his manager. Rather than giving John a pat on the back and then promptly forgetting about it, you recognize what he told you to be a milestone event in his life. You shake his hand sincerely and say, "Congratulations, John! What's your baby's name?"

"John, Jr.," he beams.

"And how's Mama doing?" you ask.

"Mary's fine," he says.

"Tell me about John, Jr.," you continue.

"Well, he's a big boy. He reminds me of my Dad, Bill. I figure John, Jr. will play linebacker for the Cowboys one day," John winks, laughs, as he moves along to shake another hand.

Later, preferably shortly after this conversation, you go to your *Milestone Box* and you write at the top of the card the date of the milestone event—in this case, the baby's birth: "June 21, 2003." Skip down a few lines on the same index card and write the employee's name, *"John Gallagher."* Skip down a few more lines and describe the relevant and important information you gleaned from the conversation, which was what?

> *"John's wife, Mary, had a little boy today, John, Jr. John says he looks like his dad, Bill, and commented he was "big, and would probably play for the Cowboys one day."*

In this one short conversation, you recorded a milestone event and identified several of the most credible connections in John's life: birth of a child, name of his wife, and name of his father.

In short, to be effective, you don't need to spy or pry to learn. Don't worry if your *Milestone Box* does not contain every life-changing event in every one of your employees' lives six months from the day you begin. It won't happen. Don't force it. The information you need will come to you. Your job is to be open to listening to spontaneously shared accounts of your employees' milestones, being attentive, perceiving them accurately, communicating your understanding and appropriately responding.

Step Three: Write Your Milestone Cards, End Of Day, Date First

When you write *Milestone Cards* is your decision, but we have found it is best accomplished at the same time each day. We have found those managers who allot about fifteen minutes at the end of each workday to write their *Milestone Cards* entries into their *Manager's Journal* (Chapter 10), and their *Care Cards* (Chapter 11) gather more important information than those who record willy-nilly.

We also have found that the end of your workday is the best time to write *Milestone Cards*. Why? The events of the day are still fresh in your mind. If you wait until the next morning, you put sleep and another twelve hours or so between the events and your recollection of them. And, if you're like us, once you've slept, you've pretty much cleansed your short-term memory. (Alcohol doesn't help your memory, either, so before you leave work, before you sleep, and before you have that evening cocktail, write your *Milestone Cards*!) Or even better, do like some managers who don't trust their memory even to the end of the day. They carry a small notebook in their pocket and note the milestones they learn during the day and then transfer them to *Milestone Cards* at the end of their work day.

Now, let's assume that you have reached the end of your workday, are sitting alone in your office, cubicle, or in the Credible Connections room your company has set aside for this purpose. You have taken a few moments and a deep breath or two and cleared your mind of widget counts, spreadsheets, broken equipment, and severed Internet connections. Once your blood pressure is back within range of the nearest speed limit, you concentrate and relive your workday, seeing in your mind's eye the day unfold again. You will see the faces and hear the conversations, especially the important ones, because you went into the experience knowing what you were looking for: milestones in your employees' lives. Perhaps you pull out that little pocket notebook which aids your recollection. Perhaps you just close your eyes and let it all come to you. However you do it, you do it, and you do it every day at or near the same time. In six weeks, creating *Milestone Cards* will become a habit, a very effective habit.

"But, what do I write?" you ask. "Just the facts, ma'am." After noting the date of the event, the name of the employee, you jot a short description of the event you wish to remember. Here's another *Milestone Card* written by John Gallagher's manager:

6/23/03
John Gallagher
John's wife, Mary, gave birth to John, Jr. today, their first child. John says he looks just like his father, Bill Gallagher. He said, "he's built like a football player," and joked that "he's the next start linebacker for the Dallas Cowboys."

Date, employee, event.

It is that easy. By recognizing that a milestone event was unfolding, listening attentively and asking a question or two that indicates his genuine interest, John's manager not only documented the milestone event of birth, but also learned the name of John's wife and his father, as well as an important anecdote that will always draw John back to the event; that is, his quip about John, Jr. growing up to be a Dallas Cowboys football player. That's plenty, as you will see, when John's manager follows up on this milestone event later.

Step Four: Insert Milestone Cards Under Anniversary And/Or Follow-Up Dates

Your *Milestone Card* is complete. It is now time to file it in your *Milestone Box*. The obvious question arises, "Where do I file it?" Answer: File it under the date on which you wish to *follow up* with the employee. In the case of a birth of a child, you will likely want to follow up annually, and so you would file the card under the "June" tab. A year hence, when sorting through your June cards and inserting the 1-31 tabs into the active month for ease of reference, you would file it under "23" for the 23rd of that month.

In other situations, you will want to follow up more often than annually. For example, what if all of the same events occurred except that John's wife Mary had a difficult birthing experience and remained in the hospital? John would be, of course, concerned, and his manager's *Milestone Card* might look like this:

6/23/01
John Gallagher
John's wife, Mary, gave birth to John, Jr. today, their first child. John says he looks just like his father, Bill Gallagher. He said, "he's built like a football player," and joked that "he's the next start linebacker for the Dallas Cowboys." John is concerned, however, because Mary had an unexpected Ceasarian section and must remain in the hospital for another 2 or 3 days.

Most certainly, John's manager would want to follow up on Mary's condition sooner than a year from the birth of John, Jr. Let's assume that he decides to follow up with John three days hence. He would simply file the card under index tab "26" under the current month's tab. As he reviews his *Milestone Cards* on the 26th, he will come across this *Milestone Card* and will follow up with John about Mary on that date. Assuming all is well, he would then file the card behind the "June" tab for use the following June 23.

Some events require multiple reminders. For example, if a manager knows his employee has a close family member who has been given three months to live, it would be not helpful to file the card in on the date the illness is discovered, with a view of following up annually. After all, the odds are long that by the time that date rolls around again, the funeral will be but a memory. Far more helpful would be to place the card ahead one week, check with the employee, and then file the card again another week into the future until there is no further use for the card, at which time it can be discarded.

Step Five: Don't Sit Down Each Morning Before You "Do Your Cards"

Just as the end of your workday is a time of reflection, a time to record the milestone events in your employees' lives, the beginning of your day is the time to execute upon them, to use them with the goal of creating relationships. Remember Hank, our creative young president who would not sit down in the morning until he had "done his cards"? Follow his example and you will be effective, too.

At the beginning of each workday, take out your *Milestone Box,* review those filed under the tab for that day, and decide who you are going to talk with and what you are going to talk about. On June 23, 2004, John Gallagher's *Milestone Card* will miraculously appear in his manager's *Milestone Box* and his manager will know that this day is one he needs to remember. It was a milestone in John's life. He will relive the event hundreds, perhaps thousands of times before his life's journey ends.

John's manager will read the card that morning, and although the *Milestone Card* may not recount every word said during their conversation a year before, John's manager will recall the conversation as if it had happened the day before. The *Milestone Card* acts as the pointer to the manager's memory of the conversation. The memory was there all along, but out of mind's reach. Think of your *Milestone Cards* as your directory track for those events that would not otherwise be remembered.

John's manager approaches John on June 23, 2004.

"How's John, Jr.? Having a birthday party this weekend for him?" his manager asks.

"Yep, sure are!" John exclaims with joy and surprise. "Hey, how did you know it was John, Jr.'s birthday?"

"I try to remember the things that are important. I remember when Billy, my first son, was a year old. It's just like it was yesterday, and he's twenty now."

"Isn't that the truth? I remember bringing him home from the hospital just like it was yesterday."

"So, you signed him with the Cowboys yet?"

Smiling, John replies as he, too, remembers the conversation from the year before. "Not yet, but he's still a big guy. He's wearing 18 month sizes at a year old!"

"And Mary's doing well? I remember she had a hard time of it."

"Oh, yeah, she's doing great. In fact, next week's her birthday. Glad you reminded me."

"No problem. What day next week? We'd like to send her a card."

"Next Thursday. I'm sure she'd appreciate it."

"Take care."

"You bet. And, hey boss, thanks for remembering."

Conversations like this occur in workplaces all across America everyday and have their genesis in a single card that resides in a cheap plastic index card box. The *Milestone Cards* provide the knowledge that is essential to develop the empathy required to create meaningful relationships. John and his manager are well on their way to knowing each other better, of caring about each other because they now have something important to share.

But you may ask, "How will John's manager remember to send a card to Mary?" Easy. He will create a new *Milestone Card* that evening.

6/23/04
Birthday of John's wife, Mary.

As John's manager reviews his *Milestone Cards* every morning, always looking three to five days ahead, he will see Mary's birthday and it will trigger him to acknowledge (and even remind John) of his wife's birthday. As you'll see in Chapter 11, he'll also write a *Care Card* wishing Mary a happy birthday and perhaps have everyone in John's department sign it.

Whether it is a joyous event such as a birth or significant accomplishment, or a painful event such as a death or divorce, the *Milestone Box* is utilized in the same way. The manager listens for milestone events in his employees' lives. When he learns of a milestone event, he records it on a *Milestone Card* and notes at the top of the card the date on which the event occurred. He then files the card either on that date (for follow-up a year hence), or a preceding date on which he wishes to follow up.

Here is another example:

9/15/01
John Gallagher
Death of John's mother, Sarah. John was close to his mother, who he described as "strong and supportive," and recalled a time when he wanted to drop out of high school and go to work because their family had money problems. His mother would not let him give up his education and took a second job to get them through.

This is an example of a *Milestone Card* that would best be filed for follow-up a few days from the event—perhaps on the day John is scheduled to return from funeral leave. After acknowledging John's loss, expressing regret, and remembering what John had told him about his mother, the good manager will ask whether there is anything he can do for John or his family—and he will mean it. If the relationship is such that another follow up with John is appropriate a month hence, the *Milestone Card* will be filed under the October tab, later to be assigned an appropriate follow-up date by the manager. (Remember: As you begin a new month, shift the 1-31 index tabs to the new month and sort the milestone cards of that month by date for ease of use.) Regardless of the number of interim follow-ups, the manager eventually files the *Milestone Card* behind the month tab to designate a follow up on the yearly anniversary date of the event. In this case, the manager will then file the card behind the September tab in order to be able to touch John again on the anniversary of the death of his mother, for surely John will both value and appreciate a sincere expression of care and concern then, too.

High Tech Alternatives

Can milestones be recorded electronically?

Yes, the *Milestone Box* has been automated. But, experience tells us that the *Milestone Box* is rarely automated effectively except by those who have been successful in using it manually first.

Why?

First, the adage that you cannot automate anything you cannot do manually is true. Perhaps it is true because it is easier for most managers to understand a manual system that they touch, manipulate, and use than a system where many of the functions are hidden from them. The managers to whom we have explained the *Milestone Box* who have dispensed with the box, tabs, and cards and gone straight to their planners or computers have generally come up short because they never understood the system.

Second, "nothing is less instructive than a machine."[cxxviii] This is especially so with computers, where most of the manipulation occurs out-of-sight, in the background, shielding the user from the ministerial, but in some cases also the essential. In short, it helps to have seen the machine work before trying to reinvent it.

Third, we have yet to meet the manager who backs up his computer data with the regularity necessary to insure that milestone events don't eventually make their way to the bit-bucket—that place in cyberspace where our data resides after it is lost. Once managers know and express an interest in the milestone events of their employees, follow-up is not an option; it is essential, and no employee will find "I had a hard disk problem" as a good enough reason to have forgotten his or her wedding anniversary you seemed so interested in the year before.

So, do it the right way and utilize your *Milestone Box* for six months to a year, learn how it works, make your own substantive and logistic modifications along the way, and after it has proven itself, if you want to automate it, go for it. We have, and you can learn more about the automated systems available at *www.crediblyconnect.com*.

Following Up On Milestone Events: What To Do, What To Say

"When a milestone comes up, what should I do? What should I say?"

A good question, and the answer is simple. "Say what you *feel*. Just make sure you feel it first." In other words, instead of jabbering incoherently or engaging in a stream of consciousness dialog, or even worse, using the words of others, ask yourself these two questions before following up on a milestone event:

- "Based on what I know about this person, if I were him, what would I feel right now?"
- "If I were feeling what he feels, what expression would give me the most joy, comfort, or consolation?"

Ask and answer those two questions before following up, and you will rarely, if ever, go wrong.

A Pat On The Back: Touching Has Gotten A Bad Name

Words are not the only way to recognize milestone events. A pat on the back, a shake of the hand, and even a hug were once common in the workplace. Then along came "The Clarence Thomas/Anita Hill Show" and suddenly legislators and lawyers convinced America that every touch between the genders was filthy and evil, especially if guys were doing the touching. Tales of the lurid riveted America and pats on the butt became daily fodder of newspapers and television. Sexual harassment became a cottage industry that sent many lawyers' children to fine private schools. Trainers and HR-types jumped on the bandwagon to justify their existence, each predicting hideous doom, courtesy of testosterone. Before they were muzzled by an already overburdened judicial system, nearly every manager in America was convinced that any touching of an employee was surely his E-ticket to hell. In the course of it all, men were told to leave their common sense at home, and most of them did, no longer being able to distinguish a pat on the back from a pat on the butt. Nonsense repeated became truth for the herd. Many an average guy witnessed the oftentimes-indiscriminate legal carnage, and in sheer terror they drew the line at touching anyone for any reason at any time.

In so doing, managers discarded an important management and relationship-building tool: the human touch. From birth to death, humans do better mentally, physically, and emotionally if they are touched by and touch others. Infants who are touched and held with care and affection during their formative years grow up to be more emotionally stable than those who are treated as lepers.

Physicians have discovered that touching and healing are indelibly connected. One surgeon tested the theory. He decided that he would divide his surgical patients into two groups. He would speak to one group after surgery, but would stand away from them and not touch them at all, unless it was required to examine them. With the other group, he would pat their hands, hold their hands, or put his hand on their shoulder as he spoke. He carefully stayed the same length of time with each patient. When they were discharged, the patients who were touched believed the physician visited with them twice as long as he really had, favorably remarked on the quality of their care, and most went home earlier than expected; they healed faster. The untouched didn't believe the doctor had stayed as long as he had stayed, went home about the time they were expected to go home, and had no comments about their care.

Irrational fears of being labeled a "sexual predator" aside, we know that a pat on the back feels great to someone who has achieved a goal or accomplished something of which they are proud or valued as a physical expression of sympathy. Most people even appreciate a hug every now and then from those who care. However, touching always requires use of judgment. Good managers recognize their "untouchables," and don't touch the few who are uncomfortable being touched by anyone except perhaps close friends or relatives. They are recognizable, most letting you know up front that they don't want to be touched. For these, and for now, you have to leave touching in your toolbox of relationships. But, for a great majority of employees, whether it's a milestone of joy or sorrow, a kind touch is often more than just appropriate; it is needed.

The Family: Connecting To Their Most Important Connection: Loved Ones

As we mentioned, when we ask managers "What is the most important thing, person, or dynamic in your life?" nearly all respond "My family." Even irrepressible and unapologetic workaholics who wouldn't recognize their own families on wanted posters still dutifully plea, "My family is the most important thing in the world to me." You are not different, and neither are your employees. Their families are, likewise, the most important people in their lives, and if you want to connect with your employees, you must connect with their families. In order to do that, you must first know their names. It is hard to sound sincere asking, "John, how's your kid?" You see John doesn't think of Lisa, his beautiful little 4-year-old in her pink Sunday dress, as being just a "kid." Neither should you. Learn the names of your employees' immediate family: husband, wife, children, significant other, and any one else living under the same roof. You can do this by telling your employee that you want to get to know him better. Ask him about his family. Most people are proud of their children and will tell you all you want to know—and more. Get their names, write them down, and get their birth dates, because that is how you are going to find them in your *Milestone Box.* If the employee asks you "Why?" tell them the truth. Tell them that you have gotten into a good habit of sending best wishes on birthdays and you want his family to know that you care and value him.

Written Recognition

Individual recognition, peer recognition—is there any room for other recognition? Absolutely! Take a look up the corporate food chain. There's always Big Boss, Bigger Boss, and Biggest Boss. They may be too busy to keep a *Milestone Box,* or at least believe they are too important, but first-line managers can recognize important events on the Boss's behalf. Send a note to Big Boss praising your employee who is deserving of praise, and copy your employee. He might actually take the time to give your employee a pat on the back, and if he doesn't, don't worry about it. The important person in his work life—you—already has.

Also, write the employee directly. Personal cards and letters have been long used to express care and concern for others. Writing not only illustrates the existence of our care for each other, it causes it to exist. Whether it is individual recognition, peer recognition, or recognition from Big Boss, nothing says you care more for another than your words written in your own hand.

We will examine how to acknowledge employees effectively with the *Care Card* in Chapter 11. You will learn that it is interdependent with your *Milestone Box,* as is the next tool in the triad: your *Manager's Journal.*

CHAPTER 10

The Manager's Journal: Finding Common Ground

I spoke with Lorna who bid to the 3rd shift because of her son, Tom, 24- years old, who is learning-disabled and in a wheelchair and needs help getting ready for a ride to school each morning. I told her, "It must be tough," but she just smiled and replied, "Not at all. Tom is a blessing to me. It is what I want to do more than anything else."

- Manager's Journal Entry, Nora, 1st Line Supervisor, 3rd Shift, Manufacturing

THE second tool in the relationship-building triad of Credible Connections is the *Manager's Journal*, a diary of sorts in which managers identify common ground, unique characteristics, and opportunities to be of service to their employees. From common interests to assisting in personal and professional development, unique challenges to lending an ear, your *Manager's Journal* will document your efforts and personal goals to enhance relationships.

What goes into your *Manager's Journal* at the end of each workday is simple and straightforward:

(1) Identifying Unique Challenges

It has been said that life doesn't care as much for those who have been given wealth, fame, and comfort, meaning that the opportunity to find satisfaction in life is developed from the difficulties we face. Lorna, whom we mentioned at the beginning of this chapter, is an example of someone who has been given an opportunity and who has made the most of it. Lorna didn't whine about her 24-year-old learning disabled son. She would have life no other way, recognizing her gift—the opportunity to be in service to someone she cares for and who needs her help.

Lorna, likewise, presents an opportunity to Nora, her manager. Nora, who did nothing more than make a simple and obvious inquiry, now can connect to Lorna because she knows who is most important in her life. She can use what she knows in service to Lorna, who one day may need her help, whether it be a scheduling request or a shoulder to cry on. She will be able do so because she is able to see Lorna in the light of her own unique qualities and challenges.

Each of us is unique and each of us experience unique challenges. If you know the challenges faced by each of your employees, you will understand them on a different level. Your empathy will increase. You will create meaningful relationships, out of which satisfaction and happiness are born.

(2) Common Interests

Cecil is a manager in a manufacturing plant, but when he is not managing, he is racing stock cars, something he loves to talk about. Cecil has developed relationships with his employees who share his fascination with automobiles and speed, but because men are more likely to want to play with horsepower-driven toys than women, it is not surprising that Cecil was viewed more favorably by the men he supervised and less favorably by women in his department who found him "detached." Some even accused him of "favoritism." When explored further, Cecil's "favoritism" was manifested by the time he spent talking with most male employees, specifically those who shared his fascination with auto-racing.

So on one hand, Cecil was doing a good job of creating relationships by using a common interest he shared with a few employees. However, Cecil was failing to create relationships and connect with those who didn't share his avocation. He ignored common interests he had with employees who were not car buffs. Cecil, like most managers, had more than one interest in his life, and he was able, by utilizing his *Manager's Journal*, to substantially improve his relationships with those who felt left out.

How? First, Cecil sat down and completed an interest inventory. This was nothing more than a blank sheet of paper and twenty minutes alone answering this question, "What am I interested in?" Cecil came up with a list of several interests, one of which was reading fiction— particularly mystery novels. It turns out that when he was not turning wrenches in his spare time, Cecil turned the pages of Stephen King and John Grisham. By actively listening to his employees—all of his employees—he soon found that several of those who didn't care for compression and cubic inches did enjoy reading. Soon, this common interest formed a new relationship, as reflected in his *Manager's Journal*:

> *04/11/02—Just finished* Needful Things *by Stephen King and discussed it with Janice. She is crazy about Stephen King and had read this book. We had a nice chat about its commentary on materialism in our society. She said it really "woke her up" to how attached we become to our possessions and how little they really mean. She also recommended* Carrie, *King's first book that I have not read. She is going to loan me her copy.*

Cecil's common interest with Janice, once identified and shared, provided them reason to communicate, not as superior to subordinate, but as one human being to another. The common interest also provided Cecil a valuable insight into Janice by understanding her concerns about important social issues, in this case materialism and its impact on society. The recording of this employee's interests in his *Manager's Journal* gave him that opportunity.

Begin by completing your own interest inventory and then listen to your employees. You will find matches, and from there you are one step away from forming a relationship.

(3) Opportunities For Personal and Professional Development

"Rich is reluctant to move into a supervisory position, even though I have discussed it with him many times. As a leadsperson, he is supposed to work and supervise at the same time, but I find him working a lot more than teaching when someone needs help. Today I told him that I want to see him working with others more, teaching them, mentoring them, and yes, directing their work. I have given him specific goals regarding the development of his team. He didn't seem very happy about it, but he has the skill-set to supervise and Rich is the only person holding Rich back."

Manager's Journal Entry, Carlos, Production Superintendent

Development doesn't come easily for most of us. We don't want to take risks. We don't want to change. Instead, we want to be spoon-fed—to be given what we want. We want the rewards of risk without actually taking risk. Of course life doesn't work that way, and the best managers know that; just as the best parents don't do everything for their children, the best managers don't arrest the development of their employees by doing everything for them.

As one experienced manager told us, "I'm like a mama bear raising her cubs. She doesn't give them everything, but rather teaches them skills they need for survival. Then, when the cubs are ready, she chases them up a tree and she walks away, not because she has stopped caring for them, but because she does care and knows they have been prepared to survive and flourish. It is the natural order of things." The lesson is important in our relationships with others in the workplace. Every manager's duties include the development of employees—providing them opportunities and skills to survive in the workplace and to succeed. That is what Carlos did for Rich, and his effort was successful. Rich took the lead position, excelled, and ultimately accepted the position of shift supervisor, where he thrives today. Rich told us that had Carlos not "nudged" him, he would have been working on a machine forever. The only people who will push you toward success are those who know you and who care about you.

(4) Lending An Ear

Experienced managers know that because an employee recounts a problem doesn't mean they expect the manager to solve it. To the contrary, when employees share concerns with their managers, they are often not asking for advice, judgment, conversation, or comment. Rather, they just want someone to listen to them. And listening, really listening, is a mark of all great managers and all great communicators. Gay Hendricks and Gay Ludeman, in *The Corporate Mystic*,[cxxix] recount the story of a friend who went with his wife to a party where he knew no one. Rather than talking, he did nothing that evening but listen carefully and restate what each person told him. On his way home that evening, his wife told him how many people had remarked that he was powerful, charismatic, and articulate.

The best managers are sensitive to what role they are being asked to play when an employee tells them of a problem or a challenge. Sometimes, employees want their manager to be a sounding board; other times they seek advice; on other occasions they want a shoulder to cry upon; and sometimes they just want someone to listen. In most cases, when employees want a manager's advice, they will ask for it. And whether or not advice is sought, listen first, never finish the employee's sentences, don't presuppose the problem after a partial description, and don't offer up a solution unless and until the employee asks or pauses, clearly waiting for a comment or an opinion. Here's an example from a *Manager's Journal*:

> *08/23/02—Leland approached me today and was angry because one of his neighbors had borrowed his lawnmower and didn't return it. He was shocked and angry that anyone would borrow something, use it, and not return it without so much as a "thanks." He vented, and I listened.*

Leland was not looking for his manager's commentary, agreement, or advice. He just wanted to express his frustrations, and his manager took the fifteen seconds to let him have his say, to let Leland utter his polemic on the importance of sharing (and returning) in being a good neighbor. Leland's manager wrote it in his *Manager's Journal* because he sensed the event hit one of Leland's "hot buttons." One day, he thought, "I might be able to help Leland by recalling this strongly held belief." And he was right.

> *02/03/04 – Bill (1st shift supervisor) came to me today and said that Allison (whom he supervises) has been complaining that Leland (3rd shift) has been leaving the work area a mess, that the tools are scattered and she often spends an inordinate amount of time trying to find them. I found an 08/02/02 entry on Leland and recalled a conversation I had with him about a neighbor who didn't return his lawnmower. I approached him about the problem with Allison and likened leaving tools scattered to not returning them, i.e., that just like his lawnmower, Allison should have the tools "returned" so she can use them—that they are "joint owners" of these tools. He was surprised I remembered his story, and he seemed moved. I confirmed with Bill that I had spoken to Leland and asked him to get back to me on whether or not this issue had been resolved.*

Leland's manager was able to access a long forgotten conversation, one in which he just "lent an ear," to correct a work-related situation. Absent the entry into his *Manager's Journal*, the best Leland's manager could have done was given a directive: "Stop leaving your work area a mess, Leland!" As a relationship-based manager, he knew that getting Leland's buy-in was more likely to net positive results and that using Leland's own prior experience was the best avenue to achieve that buy-in.

(5) Your Relationship Goals

Your *Manager's Journal* finally acts as the place to establish and document your goals for the development of relationships with each of your employees.

> *"Re: Judy Jones. Judy recently joined our department. She is very quiet and keeps to herself. My goal is to discover something in which she has an interest in the next 30 days."*
> - Janice, Line Supervisor, Manager's Journal Entry

By writing down her goal, Janice made a commitment to herself, one that she could not later deny, forget, or justify not doing. After taking a few minutes and discovering Judy's interests, one of which was photography, Janice set another goal for the following 30 days to pursue that interest by bringing some of her own photographs to work to discuss them with Judy and to get her opinion on how she might improve her photography, all with a view of establishing a relationship.

Unique challenges, common interests, personal and professional development, lending an year, and your goals to develop relationships are what should be recorded in your *Manager's Journal,* the mechanics of which are easy and straightforward to setup and maintain.

The Mechanics Of The Manager's Journal

Setting Up Your Journal

Like your *Milestone Box*, your *Manager's Journal* is easy to create, easy to maintain, and easy to use. You need a three-ring binder, dividers, and a stack of notebook paper. Each employee's name is written on one divider, because, in fact, the *Manager's Journal* is more appropriately labeled *My Employees' Journals.* Behind each employee's divider, place several sheets of blank notebook paper. That binder and a pen are all the physical tools you need to get started.

Maintaining Your Manager's Journal

As with the *Milestone Box*, the most common question about the *Manager's Journal* is "What should I write?" In your *Manager's Journal,* you will focus on and record:

- employee challenges,
- common interests you share with each of your employees,
- personal and professional development opportunities in which you may be able to assist your employees,
- occasions when you lend an year or provide input to an employee on an issue the employee deems important, and
- your goals to develop relationships.

Of course not every challenge, not every complaint, and not every common interest merits recording. Learning to distinguish between the sublime and the meaningless requires you to follow these 5 steps, which conclude with the recording of helpful information for later reflection and use:

1. *Listen.* Too many managers *hear* what their employees are saying but don't actually *listen* to what is being said. Unless the issue is on their own radar screen—that is, something important to the manager—too many of us let the observations and commentary of our employees go in one ear and out the other. It is a formula for failure if meaningful relationships are your goal. Listening is a skill that requires you to be able to quiet your mind and thereby able to listen without competition.

2. *Be open*. Let your employees know that you are ready to listen when they are ready to talk. Don't assume they know that. Tell them, "Yes, I'd like to hear about that," and when they speak, stop, look them in the eye, and put everything else you are thinking about to the side. On those occasions when you are simply too busy to listen, schedule a time to get back to the employee, and get back to her. Even if the employee misunderstands your intent and says, "No, it's not that important," you reply, "No, it is important and I'd like to hear it and help you if I can." Carry a little notepad in your pocket (the same one you use to note milestones for later recording in your *Milestone Box*), note the listening opportunity you have rescheduled, and get back to the employee at the agreed upon time.

    If you have heretofore been closed to your employees, intentionally or negligently, getting them to open up may take a little time and effort, but when employees find they have your ear and your undivided attention, they will begin communicating; you will learn more about them, leading to empathy, and ultimately to the development of relationships.

3. *Listen For Distillation*. Even though you listen intently and openly, you will find every anecdote doesn't have a point. Every comment isn't important. Every opinion isn't genuinely held. Indeed, most talk is just filling silence. That doesn't make it wrong, but it doesn't make it meaningful, either. A good way you can tell the difference is to listen for what we call "distillation," which means important conclusions and judgments your employees take away from their experiences, or the experiences of others. You will find that whether it is a unique challenge or a common interest, you can tell how important it is in their lives by simply listening for the "distillation." Specifically, listen for these affirmations:

    > "I believe..."
    > "I feel..."
    > "I sense..."
    > "It is true that..."
    > "I have no doubt that..."
    > "Rest assured that..."
    > "I have faith that..."
    > "I like..."
    > "I hate..."

These introductions generally denote importance and are worth recording.

4. *Inquire*. "All men are rotten!" Angela exclaims to her manager. Without more, her manager does not know whether that is a strongly held belief or just the result of last night's tiff with her husband or boyfriend. It is important for her to be able to separate sincere belief from hyperbole.

    "Why do you say that?" Angela's manager inquired. To that question came a response, one that revealed the basis of the belief. "Because John didn't take out the garbage," is obviously different than "because John beat me just like my last husband did."

    In most situations, asking "Why do you feel that way?" is the question sufficient to start a flow of facts from which an important perspective has developed, and it will become clear to the listening manager whether what is being said is a sincerely held belief or merely an epithet, a throwaway line, a momentary self-correcting lapse of reason.

5. *Record.* "Is it really necessary to record your relationship goals? Every time we hear that question, we're reminded of the study of the members of a 1950s Yale graduating class who were surveyed throughout their lives. Interestingly, only 3 percent of them developed written goals for their lives when they left college. Thirty years later, that 3 percent was worth more than the other 97 percent put together.

Whether financial success or success in building relationships, writing makes us think more carefully and be more specific, so that the act of writing results in a greater personal commitment, its being a promise we make to ourselves.

Once again, what should you record? Record sincere, strongly held beliefs, whether they are about personal or professional development, interests, or challenges, and the factual foundations for those beliefs, usually in the form of anecdotes. The challenge, interest, or goal about which an employee expresses an opinion or belief must be significant, but the significance is to be evaluated from their perspective, not yours. "I believe it will rain today" turns out to be insignificant. "I believe the CEO lied to us in the company meeting" is very significant, whether or not it is true. Some statements are not so easy to categorize, and in the beginning, managers should err on the side of recording too much, rather than too little.

The Milestone Box and Manager's Journal Distinguished: Fact vs. Distillation

Some managers initially experience problems distinguishing information they should record on *Milestone Cards* from that properly recorded in their *Manager's Journal*. The easiest way to make the distinction is to remember that the photographic lens of the *Milestone Box* captures the most important *events* in a life, to include the significant emotional events and milestone events we discussed in Chapter 9. The *Manager's Journal,* on the other hand, records unique challenges, common interests, personal and professional development opportunities, lending your ear to employee problems and challenges, usually expressed through their distillation of life events. In some cases, these rise to the level of milestone events, and as we will discuss in Chapter 12, each of the tools is interdependent and synergistic with the others, and they are more powerful when they are used together.

Manager's Journal: Techniques

As with the *Milestone Box*, entries into the *Manager's Journal* are best recorded at the conclusion of your workday, when the conversations are still fresh in your mind. If you don't trust your memory for a full day, don't forget that small notepad in your pocket and make notations and reminders during each day that your can use later to enter into your *Manager's Journal* and your *Milestone Box.*

Like the *Milestone Box*, there are high-tech alternatives to the pen and paper of the *Manager's Journal* which can be implemented company-wide. But until your company adopts an automated system of credible connections, we recommend keeping it simple. For most managers, that means using a three-ring notebook, tabs, and notebook paper, with each employee assigned a tab under which events, thoughts, expressions, and beliefs are noted.

Remember: Manager's Journal entries are filed by employee, the opposite of the *Milestone Box*, in which entries—the *Milestone Cards*—are filed by date.

Using the Manager's Journal—"What Should I Do With the Information Once I Have It?"

The uses of the information contained in your *Manager's Journal* are as varied as the employee beliefs, attitudes, and opportunities recorded there, but because there is no similar "tickler" system in your *Manager's Journal* as exists in your *Milestone Box*, you will need to establish a methodology of review. Most managers we know set aside a few extra minutes at the end of each week to examine the entries on one employee cover-to-cover, highlighting or mentally noting the important, relevant, and consistent. A manager with twenty-five employees under her supervision, for example, would have the benefit of a complete review of his *Manager's Journal* notations on each employee twice per year, assuming he reviews one employee's entries each week.

Different managers have adapted the *Manager's Journal* in different ways. Perhaps flexibility is its strongest feature. Managers who have used the *Manager's Journal* a year or more tell us they have found it useful in the following circumstances:

- Watching The Employee's "Video" When Nothing Makes Sense

"Bill is a great employee, a genuinely decent person," observed Larry, his manager. "We struck up a good relationship where none existed. But then—WHAM! Bill's attitude hit the bricks. He dragged around, clearly unhappy, and seemed to want to take everyone else down with him. I asked him about it but he withdrew. It didn't make any sense, so I went to my *Manager's Journal* and found something interesting. It seems that Bill was divorced about a year before his attitude went downhill, and coincidentally, it was the anniversary of his divorce that corresponded to the deterioration of his attitude. I approached him on that basis and he opened up. It was a divorce he didn't want, one that he still grieves."

Unique challenges are always recorded in the *Manager's Journal* and they will help you put together an employee puzzle that otherwise would remain unsolved and your employee without help.

- Motivating Others with Stories—Their Own

Great communicators are great storytellers. Great leaders are, too. Psychologist Howard Gardner observed that the key characteristic distinguishing exceptional leaders is their ability to create and tell effective, cohesive, compelling anecdotes. Most of us don't remember statistics, but we do remember stories, and we share them to teach others what we have learned. Stories act as a proof of the precepts and propositions that follow. Researchers from Xerox PARC found that learning was made more memorable if the point to be made was embedded in a story. Significantly, no stories are more meaningful and cogent to us than our own.

In the workplace, employees regularly share their stories with each other and with their managers. The careful manager listens and determines whether the story that is being told draws a conclusion or makes a point. If so, and the point or conclusion is significant, it should be noted in your *Manager's Journal*, for it is often of assistance in the future. Here's another example of a manager who was able to lend assistance in the professional development of one employee simply because he remembered a story:

> *03/14/01—Lanny told me a story today about his son, Tim. Tim had wanted to play baseball since he was old enough to walk and talk. When Tim was six years old, he started in T-ball. He was disappointed to tears that he couldn't hit the ball like most of the other kids on his team. After the first few games, he wanted to quit, but Lanny asked him to give it the season before he decided. Each day after work, Lanny took him out and they would tee the ball up and Tim would take swing after swing. After a month or so, he got the hang of it and did fine. Now, ten years later, Tim is a star high school baseball player and is being recruited by colleges. Lanny is one proud papa!*
>
> *- Manager's Journal, William, QC Manager*

William had no idea how that story might be useful in service to Lanny when he recorded it in his *Manager's Journal*, but he sensed its importance, because Lanny distilled the story into a life-lesson: Never give up! More than a year later, a synchronous event occurred.

> *06/19/02—Lanny was promoted to Senior Inspector a month ago and is having a hard time of it. He is learning that inspecting and being responsible for the inspections of others takes different skills. He came to me yesterday and wanted to take a demotion back to his old spot. I told him I'd give it some thought and get back to him. I found a Journal entry of 03/14/01 and approached Lanny today, and talked about Tim and how he kept swinging and missing and wanted to quit, but there was someone in his life who cared enough to help him become a success. I told Lanny that if he would let me, I would like to make him a success and told him that we'd practice together. He smiled and said he'd give it his all.*
>
> *- Manager's Journal, William, QC Manager*

Had William not been observant, not been listening effectively, Lanny would have been left with the oh-so-typical, "Hang in there, Lanny. I know you can do it!" Lanny's story was, without a doubt, more effective in helping him over his professional hurdle. Lanny's story was a metaphor for success and how it is obtained—a story he had experienced, and from it he distilled a meaning. William simply recognized the event Lanny had shared earlier as being significant, recorded it, and later used it effectively.

- Searching For Themes: Endemic Issues Of The Workplace

Over time, the *Manager's Journal* becomes a treasure trove of employee problems, challenges, opinions, interests, and observations. Each entry is unique to individual employees; however, work-related issues are sometimes shared. The observant manager, when reviewing his *Manager's Journal*, looks for issues that may be affecting more than one employee to include problems with corporate policies, procedures, specific managers or other employees, as well as wage and benefit issues. As you will see in Chapter 12, we recommend that managers come together on a regular basis to discuss work-related issues that appear to affect or concern more than one of their employees. In many cases, these issues span an entire workforce and demand institutional attention.

In answer to the question we often receive from Human Resources departments: "Doesn't this duplicate our employee survey?" No, it does not. Typical employee surveys suffer from at least two structural drawbacks not shared by the *Manager's Journal*. First, the questions in most employee surveys *assume* the problems. If the survey developer misses an issue altogether or questions are formulated too broadly to identify the issues behind employee opinion, the answer is interesting but unusable, *e.g.,* the answer to a typical survey question, "How do you rate the upper management of this company?" Employees may answer interpreting "upper management" to include "my supervisor," and if the reviewer of the survey does not know that, he may come to erroneous conclusions. While some companies follow up surveys with employee meetings, many employees refuse to participate, embarrassed to speak in front of their contemporaries, assuming nothing will happen anyway based on past experience, or fearing management retribution.

Second, formal employee surveys are not completed in real time. Rather, they are a snapshot of how employees feel about certain issues on the day the survey is completed. The *Manager's Journal,* on the other hand, reflects employee opinion over a period of time, as is thus often more reflective of reality, like a videotape is over a snapshot. A good example is the amount employees must pay for their employee medical insurance, either via premium, deductible, or co-pay. At the beginning of a new plan year when every employee is responsible for a new out-of-pocket co-pay, the issue affects more employees. If employees are facing increased out-of-pocket costs at the time the survey is taken, the plan will get an "F." But throughout the year, as more employees reach their maximum co-pay, individually or as a family, and the insurance plan begins picking up 100%, employee opinion may rise dramatically.

Depending on when the survey is taken, employee opinion on this and other important issues may, and often does, differ. The *Manager's Journal,* on the other hand, is more like a videotape of employee opinion and will reflect which issues are hot, which are not, and why. This is not to say that many of the work-related issues in the *Manager's Journal* will not be reflected in employee surveys. They will. The point is only that employee surveys, rich in detail but locked in time, are no substitutes for the less detailed but more fluid *Manager's Journal.*

- Keeping the Main Thing the Main Thing: A Tool to Build Relationships

A former law partner was fond of saying, "The main thing is to keep the main thing the main thing." The *Journal*'s main thing is to build relationships. However, as with many products, unintended, yet positive, byproducts result.

One byproduct of the *Manager's Journal* is to provide relationship-building models to others. That is, a manager's empathetic, helping behavior, initiated by the *Manager's Journal,* acts as a model for employee behavior and often enhances employees' empathy for others via behavioral reciprocity. On reflection, we should have anticipated this result, since research shows that when teachers (trainers, experimenters, etc.) model desired values, students are more likely to adopt these values than when they are merely exhorted to behave in certain ways. Empathy generated from behavior-modeling leads to an increased willingness to be open, to take another's needs into account when dealing with conflict, to engage in more effective teamwork and to experience greater job satisfaction. In other words, with the tools you build not only better employees, but better people, and become a better manager in the process.

The good manager keeps behavioral reciprocity in mind, not as an end but as a naturally occurring product of authority used well. The *Manager's Journal* provides a tool to model empathetic, positive, relationship-building behavior. Understand that how you use what you know will rub off on your employees, whether you use it well, poorly, or not at all. To that end, some managers also use this tool to track their own thoughts. If they feel anger at a situation or a person, they note it. If they fail to exhibit patience, they note it. It seems the mere knowledge of our thoughts helps us to control them.

Improper Uses Of The Manager's Journal

George Elliott once observed that "...knowledge is power, but it is a power reined by scruple, having a conscience of what must be and what may be...." Just as a hammer can be used to build a home, so can it be used to destroy one. The same is true for each of the tools we describe in this book, especially the *Manager's Journal.*

If knowledge is the basis of power, then the *Manager's Journal* makes you powerful. And, if "power tends to corrupt,"[cxxx] as Lord Acton observed more than a century ago, then the *Manager's Journal* is a formidable weapon in the hands of the wrong manager, just as it a formidable builder of relationships in the hands of the right one. Thus as with any powerful tool, it must be, as Elliott admonished, "reined by scruple" through conscience.

To that end, there are uses to which the *Manager's Journal* can be put that belie its intended purpose, even to the point of making relationships more difficult to form or nurture. Here are some improper uses for the *Manager's Journal* which we advise against, and our rationale for each:

- *Discipline.* Employees soon notice a difference in a manager who utilizes the *Manager's Journal.* They note a heightened level of awareness. Most employees do not "look the proverbial gift horse in the mouth," but rather enjoy the new-found attention and are satisfied to see where it leads. A few, however, will ask "Why are you doing this? Are you writing this down? And, if so, what do you use it for?" As we have said before, you should answer truthfully, and the truth should be, "Because I care and I want to establish a better relationship with you." Yet whatever the manager answers, the jury will remain out to the inquiring employee until he sees how it is, in fact, being used.

For this reason, the *Manager's Journal* should never be used as a disciplinary tool, a place to note performance or behavioral deficiencies with a view toward using that information later to discipline or discharge. When discipline becomes necessary, most workplaces have a system in place to effectuate documentation of poor performance and inappropriate behavior. That system, not the *Manager's Journal*, should be used to implement discipline, and the two should never be confused.

- *Faults and Fault-Finding.* The French writer Rochefoucauld said, "If we had no faults of our own, we [would] not take so much pleasure in noticing those in others."[cxxxi] It is an axiom every manager should understand before assuming management responsibility, and most certainly before using the *Manager's Journal.* With the knowledge of an employee's weakness—personal or professional—the manager is in a position of diminishing the employee by noting his weaknesses to him, chapter and verse. To so use the *Manager's Journal* makes it a tool of destruction, rather than creation. A manager who is tempted to utilize the contents of the *Journal* to prove himself correct by proving others wrong is using the tool inappropriately.

- *Gossip.* Scandal and gossip are present in every workplace—some more than others. The office gossip is often one who has access to facts, at least some of them, and is willing to tell all he knows to whoever will listen. It is the gossip's way of being powerful. But gossips in any workplace are rarely respected and cease to interest others after the shock of the current scandal wears off. More importantly, gossips are never trusted, if only because everyone knows they may be the gossip's next topic of conversation. Unfortunately, the *Manager's Journal* makes the manager the potential "king of gossip" if he utilizes the tool to "kiss and tell," another use contrary to its purpose. Except under conditions which we will describe, the *Manager's Journal* should be entitled to the privacy to which the employee would accord it if he had written it himself.

- *Breach Of Confidence.* While we encourage managers to err on the side of writing too much rather than too little in the *Manager's Journal,* there are exceptions to what should be recorded. When an employee approaches his manager and discusses a personal matter, one they note to be "confidential," and ask and receive assurances from their manager that "what was said between us will go no further," then it should go no further. In short, if the employee desires secrecy, and after hearing what the employee has to say, the manager agrees the matter should remain between the two of them, it is inappropriate to record the conversation in the *Manager's Journal.*

- *Avoidance of Legal Pitfalls.* While the *Manager's Journal* should be considered confidential, under certain circumstances it could become public, even against the manager's wishes. There is a possibility that if your company is sued, your *Manager's Journal* could be subpoenaed or requested in discovery. This possibility, however remote, requires the prudent manager to be circumspect about writing in their *Journal* about any of the following issues:

- accusations of illegal discrimination against the company by the employee,
- allegations of injuries on the job,
- allegations of ethics or security breaches (and there are plenty of these with seventy-five percent of all workers reporting they have viewed illegal or unethical acts in their workplaces).[cxxxii]
- labor organization activity, and
- allegations by an employee that he has been asked or has performed illegal acts on behalf of the company.

In most companies, there are established ways of reporting these events and they should be followed. Questions you may have about the "thou-shalt-nots" should be referred to in-house counsel or to the Human Resources Department, especially when you have a question about legal implications.

The Manager's Journal: Your Journal Of Personal Growth

Well-used, the *Manager's Journal* is the most powerful in the triad of tools. The manager who uses the *Journal* learns and remembers the details of important employee thoughts, beliefs, challenges, feelings and interests, sees what his employees see, feels what they feel, and thereby experiences a deep empathy from which meaningful relationships naturally result, and with them a new satisfaction with work.

Managers often tell us they find it amazing to look back on their *Manager's Journals*, read their own words, and realize just how much has happened along the way—how far they have progressed both personally and professionally. It seems that recording important events in our own lives and the lives of those important to us provides a dimension beyond the spoken word, and for many managers this provides a glimpse into their own souls and spirits. We learn that life is not comprised of magnificence, glory, or notoriety; rather it is built on the everyday, the seemingly mundane that acts as the adhesive that connects us one to the other. These connective events are worth recording, worth remembering, and worth using in service to others.

With that firmly in mind, let's move on to the third and final tool in the relationship-building triad—the *Care Card*—a palpable, age-old, highly effective way to illustrate your understanding, care, compassion, and concern.

CHAPTER 11

The Care Card: A Palpable Tool To Express Care, Compassion, and Concern

Dear Bill,

I was saddened to hear about the unexpected death of your mother. Please convey our sincere regrets to your father and to your family. I remember meeting your mother, Janice, last year at our Open House. She was friendly and gracious and I know that you and others will miss her.

I lost my mother two years ago, and I understand how difficult this time is for you and your family. It is a time that you may feel the need to call on others, and I want you to call on me if there is anything I can do.

Sincerely,

John

JOHN, a supervisor, wrote this card to Bill, one of his employees. In more than 20 years of work, Bill had never received personal correspondence from any of his managers or supervisors. When Bill arrived at work after his mother's funeral, he arrived carrying this card and kept it on his desk for several days. Bill had never been demonstrative toward, nor particularly close to John, or to his co-workers, for that matter. Yet upon his return, he thanked John personally, along with every employee in his department who had likewise signed the card at John's behest. He genuinely valued the care they had exhibited during his time of grief. Bill, for the first time, viewed those with whom and for whom he worked in a different way, one that revealed a side more human and personal. Hundreds of other managers have had similar experiences.

"From just a card?" you ask. Yes, and there are good reasons why.

The Power of the Written Word

Once upon a time, not so very long ago, personal written correspondence was commonplace among people who knew and cared for each other. Putting pen to paper memorialized significant events in the lives of people close to us. Deaths, births, marriages, anniversaries, times of joy, sorrow, success, and failure were regularly acknowledged with a letter, card, or note.

That was a slower era, to be sure—a time when we had time, and *took* time, to gather our memories, thoughts, and feelings, commit them to paper, seek out an address, and place it in the mail. It was a time when social contacts were bound in custom, when we viewed ourselves not quite so individually, but as a part of a bigger whole.

More than communication of information, such writings were acts of stewardship, epigrammatic expressions and meditations given with no expectation of reward or acknowledgement other than the knowing that our kindness was valued and appreciated. Our cursive was concise, but our messages were profound symbols of our care, concern, compassion, and affection for others. They were a fundamental element in relationships a century ago and an important part of our history, one that goes back more than 3,000 years.

The Near Death of the Written Word

Writing retained its prominent place in American culture until the telephone appeared—a faster, more efficient, and interactive way to communicate. The telephone made passage of news and thoughts easy, and it was the time- saving nature of the medium that laid waste to written correspondence. Ezra Pound saw the handwriting on the wall and said as early as 1910, "The art of letters will come to an end before AD 2000... It shall survive as a curiosity."[cxxxiii] He may not have been right, but his case is looking stronger all the time.

Yet, because speaking and writing are different qualitatively, the former has been unable to wholly replace the latter. Unlike talking on a telephone, which requires no planning, thought, or even reason, writing compels us to consider the purpose of our communications and refine our thoughts, feelings and opinions before, not after, expressing them. Writing gives us time, and indeed requires us to reflect before expressing our thoughts and feelings. The telephone, on the contrary, has proven a poor substitute for insightful communication and relationship-development and often is not a communications device at all, but rather has become more like the television—something to entertain us when we are bored, something to do that is easier than working on our relationships with others. With the telephone you can dial, chatter, and listen—or not. Walk through any airport and watch people with cell phones glued to their ears who are not communicating, but are being entertained.

The weakness of the spoken word still stands in stark contrast to the quality of written communication, which is almost always more accurate and expressive of our thoughts and feelings. Even those who know nothing of letter writing and who perhaps have never written a letter understand their importance and feel their impact when they are the recipient of a well-written letter or note.

Writing and Talking: The Significant Contrast

Whether by history, experience, or intuition, each of us has learned to expect less from verbal communication with its halting starts, stops, and frequent retractions, explanations, and stream of consciousness digressions. The inane and banal are accepted as a part of the give and take of speech, and it weaknesses, not surprisingly, minimize its perceived value.

Take your birthday, for example, and consider these alternative scenarios. You assume the role of Bob. It is your birthday.

Alternative 1:

(Telephone rings)

You (Bob): Hello.

Bill: Hey, Bob, it is Bill. I'm between appointments and just wanted to wish you a Happy Birthday. Hey, did you watch the game last night? What a comeback!
You (Bob): Listen, Jim, I appreciate your calling, but I'm right in the middle of a project I have to deliver by noon. Can we chat later?

Not bad. Bill's attempt was better than forgetting Bob's birthday altogether, but put yourself in Bob's place. Did you feel special knowing that Bill took five seconds to dial your number and say "Happy Birthday"?

Alternative 2:

At your home, you receive this unexpected handwritten card in your mailbox. After dinner, when you have a few minutes of quiet time, you take it out and read it in good light over a cup of coffee.

> *Dear Bob:*
> *50? 50? That's hard to believe, my friend, if only because I remember us celebrating your and my 40th just yesterday. The next time I look up, we will both be retiring, but before that happens, I want to tell you how much I value and appreciate your support, hard work, and good nature. Happy birthday, and please pass my best along to Kathy and the kids.*
> *Best,*
> *Bill*

Did the second communication feel different from the first? Was there a difference in the quality and impact of these communications? Bill, after all, wished you a happy birthday in both scenarios, but as the recipient, did one make you feel more valued than the other? Did one illustrate empathy more than the other? Was it the letter? It has been for everyone we have ever asked.

Why? Here are some of the reasons we hear most often:

- You appreciate the effort Bill made to write a card (as opposed to the few seconds he took to dial a telephone, if he dialed at all).
- Bill's written message was more personal.
- You can share Bill's thoughts, recollections, and feelings with your spouse and family. (Liz Carpenter is right when she says "What a lot we lost when we stopped writing letters! You can't reread a phone call!")[cxxxiv]
- The letter was physical, temporal, and felt more like a gift than a message.

- When you went to the mailbox and saw a hand-addressed letter from someone you knew, you felt an expectation, an excitement.
- Receiving the letter, you felt singled out as someone worthy of a special recognition.
- In one situation, you didn't have the time to absorb the communication, and in the other you did.
- You know that no one has to write anyone else anymore, and few do, but that your manager valued you enough to do so made it special.
- You know that no response is required. (As Byron observed, "one of the pleasures of reading...letters is the knowledge that they need no answer.")

What was the difference for you? For most managers, the answer is "all of the above."

Some argue that Bill could have said the same things to Bob in his telephone conversation that he wrote in his card. Technically, that is true, but it is most unlikely that he would have done so, if only because few of us take the minute, two, or three, to prepare and gather our thoughts, reflect on the history of our relationship with another, and taste our words carefully before picking up a telephone and making a call. Instead, we let our fingers do the walking, let our mouths do the talking, and stumble through our mind dump. Written correspondence has always been a stronger medium of communication than verbal expression." Jeremy Rifkin described the difference this way: writing is "orderly, rational, and objective..." in contrast to our "oral culture [ruled by] redundancy and discontinuity in conversation."[cxxxv]

Whatever the qualitative difference between written and verbal communication, it is not wasted on the recipient of our thoughts. Jennifer Williams, in her book *The Pleasures of Staying in Touch,* draws the contrast, from the perspective of the recipient this way: "A letter is never as strident or insistent as a telephone; it has lovely manners and quietly waits on the mantel or kitchen table until the moment is right for you to hear its message. A letter," she observes, "takes into account the person to whom you are writing. It gives him or her time to digest what you have said, without interruption or embarrassment."[cxxxvi]

The obvious and important differences in written and verbal communications are not to imply that verbal connections are not important. They are. Looking an employee straight in the eye and patting him on the back and wishing him a hearty, "Happy birthday!" is a good thing, and your *Milestone Box* will help you remember to do just that. But a broad-brush verbal stroke is not a substitute for a considered writing; it is only an addition to it. The very emptiness of the paper in front of you demands that it be filled, and most people feel compelled to fill it with something meaningful and reasonably articulate, amusing, sincere, funny, and most importantly, empathetic.

Stop for a moment and recall some of the letters, cards, and notes that you have received in your life and specifically remember those that made a difference. You will make your own best argument for beginning a life of letters, notes, and cards to and for those who you feel close to or with whom you want to create a relationship.

In the workplace, we encourage managers to write their employees on specific occasions which we will identify later in this chapter. We call these writings *Care Cards*, because that is what they are—cards written by managers who care and who are willing to spend a few minutes to express care, compassion, concern, and empathy for those for whom they are responsible.

What's In It For You?

Importantly, the recipient of personal correspondence is not the only one nurtured by a well-written note. The writer, too, is enriched by the experience of writing. More than one manager, after six months of writing *Care Cards,* has told us, "I've never been able to really express myself— until now."

Because writing requires us to put our history with others into perspective—to become conscious of our thoughts, our memories, and our feelings—it requires that we examine ourselves. Memories summoned, emotions identified, writing words to express our feelings, this makes us more thoughtful, more compassionate, and more empathetic. Horace Walpole said it succinctly. "I never understand anything until I have written about it."

Writing also requires us to slow down, to cede our busyness to another time and place, and to summon ourselves from a different, more tranquil part of us. We are better able to express our true sentiments, and for some, empathy is expressed that could not have been expressed without the preparation required to write.

In the ideal world, we would write frequently to those who make our lives richer, easier, and more rewarding. Unfortunately for most managers today, the pace of modern business, as we discussed in Chapter 8, imposes duties and diversions that compete for our time, making the effort of writing, addressing, posting, and mailing personal notes to each of our employees no more realistic than remembering the names of our employees' spouses, children, and extended family. Yet remembering those names is both essential and possible via the *Milestone Box,* and as you will soon see, there is also time in your day for writing a *Care Card* or two. Here's how one manager summarized it:

> *After your program, I decided to give Care Cards a try. I was one of the "cynics" you talked about, but I told myself I'd give the program six weeks, and I did. While we don't work for an employer that prohibits or discourages meaningful relationships between managers and their employees, they have never encouraged them, either. For us, it was "optional," much like leather seats in a car—nice, comfortable, but not necessary to its operation.*
>
> *The first Care Card I wrote was to one of my employees, a real funny guy, who was ill and out a week. I told him in my card just how much we missed him and his humor, and we did! He called the day he received the card to tell me that it had made him feel better, physically and emotionally. He was actually choked up! When he returned to work, he handed me a thank you note and he shared some things with me about his family, noting that he didn't even get a card or call from his brother during his illness. I believe I helped him during his challenge, and that was the beginning of our relationship, one that makes him more satisfied at work, and me, too!*

Not All Writings Are Created Equal

Some managers wanting to use *Care Cards* worry about writing effectively. "I acknowledge important events in my employees' lives—just not in writing," more than one manager has objected. "My secretary has each of my employees' birthdays and hire dates on her computer and I sign the cards personally." If you're one of these, we will break the news to you: your employees aren't lined up at their mailboxes to read your signature. And the "my secretary handles it" cards aren't worth the postage it takes to send them. It is an all-too-common institutional substitute for the expression of a person's thoughts and feelings to another. No matter how good your secretary may be, she cannot recall your knowledge of an employee, or your feelings. Institutional correspondence is never a substitute for personal communication, nor will disruptive phone calls, group celebratory meetings, e-mail messages, in-office massages, or free beverages substitute for the sincere written message of a first-line manager.

Southwest Airlines, known for their progressive employee relations' programs, in its early days had a "corporate den mother" who would send hand-written notes of compliment or condolence to many of the company's 517 employees.[cxxxvii] Those writings helped shape that unique corporate culture.

But, don't take our word for it. You receive Christmas cards every year, don't you? Some are fancy and some are simple. Most contain pre-printed sentiments, bought and paid for expressions written by professionals, followed by a hasty signature to identify the sender.

> *"Wishing you a Merry Christmas."*
> */s/ Bill*

Still other Christmas cards sent by those mired in self-importance wholly institutionalize the process by adding a pre-printed signature.

> *"Wishing you happy holidays,*
> *Bill Johnson*
> *ABC Manufacturing Company"*

Have you received one of these gems? The fact that you rated someone's automated Christmas card list doesn't make you feel unique or special, does it?

On rare occasions, however, you may have received a hand-written Christmas card from your boss or co-worker that contained a brief paragraph or two expressing a personal thought, history, or reflection. Perhaps something along these lines...

> *Bob,*
> *During the holiday season, as we think of our families, we should not forget that we are family, too. We are a workplace family, and your contributions—including your recent redesign of our network—makes me proud, as I know it must you. Thank you, Bob, and Merry Christmas to you, Becky, Chad, and Art.*
> *-Bill*

These are three common ways Bill can express holiday wishes to his employees. If you worked for Bill, which of these cards would mean the most to you? Which are you likely to reread? Which are you likely to share with your family? Which are you likely to save? Which do you most value and appreciate? Most importantly, which is likely to enhance your relationship with Bob?

Just like cards we send to our friends and families, managers need to consider the impact of what they write to their employees. Too often, the only writing received by employees from their employers, besides the obligatory 1040 IRS form each year and a package of indecipherable 401(k) retirement materials, is the institutional straight-from-the-word-processor birthday and anniversary cards that "thank you for your [fill in the blank] years with our company." These and other significant events, like deaths in an employee's family, if acknowledged at all, are accomplished via pre-printed cards signed by "Bill" or even worse preprinted "ABC Company."

It is as if we really expect our employees to strain credulity and believe that "the company"—that disembodied legal figment of some lawyer's imagination on file in Delaware—has both the ability to feel an emotion and to write about it! These cards are a little like the proverbial "Dear John" letters: hurtful. For sure, they are wastes of postage, and do nothing to create or strengthen our relationships with those we manage.

High Speed Demands High Touch

As managers' time becomes more valuable, our time to write others is diminished. Yet while the speed of our lives makes writing more difficult, the same speed enhances the effectiveness of personal correspondence. The faster we move, the more we feel like machines and the greater our need to be assured that we are not just resources, but rather human, and valued for something more than being able to make someone else a buck.

How about e-mail? Don't even think about it as a mode of meaningful personal correspondence. Electronic mail is as impersonal as a phone call, and often more terse. Electronic mail is not writing, but talking through the fingers, often without much preparation or thought, leaving the chasm between communication and meaningful communication even wider and employees' needs for palpable personal recognition of their humanness unfulfilled.

The Care Card: Your Written Expression of Empathy

"I believe personal written recognition would help me perceive, understand, and express empathy and establish relationships with my employees, and I could give 5 minutes to it each day, but there are simply too many *impediments*," one manager said, summarizing the concerns of many others. Perhaps so, but if we can show you how you can fill this need for written recognition in a few minutes a week and eliminate all impediments, would that expenditure of time be worth your sacrifice to establish or fortify relationships with your employees? If so, read on...

The Seven Impediments to Care Cards and How To Overcome Them

The novelist William Faulkner once observed, "My own experience has been that the tools I need for my trade are paper, tobacco, food, and a little whiskey."[cxxxviii] While all that may be necessary to pen a great novel, for a short note we have found managers can generally get by without tobacco, food, and whiskey. You will need more than just a sheet of paper, however. From knowing what events to acknowledge to finding a stamp, there are hurdles to getting your thoughts out of your mind, onto paper, and into an employee's hands. Each one needs to be resolved effectively if you are to be a good and regular correspondent.

Let's look at the seven impediments we hear most often to writing *Care Cards* and how to deal with each of them.

(1) "I Don't Know What Events To Acknowledge In Writing."

Besides the obvious—birthdays and dates of hire — what other events in employees' lives should be acknowledged with *Care Cards? Answer?* Send a *Care Card* for the events that, if they happened in *your* life, you would appreciate a card from someone who cared about you. A good place to start is your list of milestone events. Again, let's categorize them. This will make it easier to understand why the events are significant and allow for easy reference.

Events: Because You Are Here

There is one date that is important in all of our lives because it celebrates the beginning of our existence:

- *Birthday*

Another date most feel to be significant is the date we were born into our workplace family:

- *Date of hire*

Both dates are important and should be personally recognized. Ironically, companies have moved away from recognition of these personal milestones in recent years. The Conference Board reports that while three-fifths of companies once honored employee birthdays and dates of hire, only one-third do so today, and less than one-fifth expect such events to figure predominately in future recognition programs.[cxxxix] In their place, and to their exclusion, exceptional performance is recognized, an unfortunate, yet telling development, one that confirms what employees already believe about their companies—that their value, in fact, is as "human resources," that their "real lives" are properly sublimated to their "work lives," the value of which is measured solely by "what have you done for me lately?"

Events: Because You Have Accomplished

While personal milestones are important, work accomplishments are important, too. What are these workplace accomplishments that a manager should recognize with a *Care Card*? They include:

- *Learning.* More employees are in school than ever before. Whether the learning takes place in-house, at a local community college or at a university, to acknowledge the pursuit of education emphasizes its importance and the sacrifices attendant with learning.
- *Teaching.* Many employees without the title of "manager" or "supervisor" are teachers and mentors of others, both personally and professionally. They, too, should be recognized.

- *Sales, Production, Quality, and Service.* Most employers acknowledge goals met in these areas, but too few managers take the time to do it personally. These are perfect opportunities for *Care Cards.*
- *Team-based accomplishments.* Companies spend untold time and dollars promoting a "team" mentality, but most rewards remain individual and exclusionary. If a team is what your company really wants, then it should reward the team, and the manager should acknowledge the team and each of its members. Whether it is a team that solves the most complex of operational problems, the team that plans the firm Christmas party or a summer picnic, or the team that assumes special responsibilities for workplace safety, if the company finds the issue to be resolved significant enough to establish a team to do it, then when the objective and attainable goals are met, the team should be rewarded and acknowledged for meeting those goals, they should include *Care Cards* from their managers.

Events: Because You Have A Family

The few rituals we have left in post-modern western society are often related to family and significant events in their lives, and therefore ours. These include:

- *Engagement to be married*
- *Marriage*
- *Birthday of spouse*
- *Birth of a child*
- *Accomplishments of family members*

In addition to happy and joyful events, some events appropriate to recognize by a *Care Card* are mired in sadness and tragedy. These are events that cause us to be at our lowest, times when we need to know that someone cares. These include:

- *Divorce*
- *Illness (personal and family)*
- *Death (of a spouse, child, parent, close family member, friend, or significant other)*

Events: Because They Care, Too!

Even our existence, tenure, accomplishments, and families do not define every significant experience in life worthy of recognition by a *Care Card.* Many employees, for example, are involved in altruistic efforts on behalf of others, *i.e.,* they are "givers," inside or outside the workplace, efforts that should be acknowledged. These include:

- *Charitable activities and contributions*
- *Public service*
- *Personal favors and good deeds, especially those for co-workers.*

Is that all? We thought so. But now, after seeing *Care Cards* used for years by thousands of creative managers, we are convinced that it is impossible to list every event in life that is appropriate to acknowledge in writing. Managers who use *Care Cards* never cease to amaze us with their creativity and compassion. If you are just starting the process and you are looking for a "bright line" test that will lead you to know whether to send a *Care Card* in a particular situation, you need only ask yourself this question:

> *If it was my experience or my accomplishment, would I appreciate a written personal acknowledgement from my manager or co-worker?*

If your answer is "yes," then write a *Care Card.*

(2) "Dates, Dates: Who Has the Dates?"

You have the dates, because most of the events appropriate to be acknowledged by a *Care Card* occur in the present moment. The date you learn of the event is the date you write the card.

> *"John's mom died today. That's why he's not here."*
> *"We're having a baby!"*
> *"My little girl is in the hospital again. I'll be absent today."*
> *"Well, I finally popped the question and guess what? I'm getting married!"*
> *"I'm getting a service award tomorrow at the department meeting."*

Write the *Care Card* that day!

(3) "I Don't Have A Card And No Time To Buy One"

No card? No problem.

You don't need a card someone else has written. You need a fresh card. You need a stack of blank cards. The best *Care Cards* always begin blank and only express your sentiment after you finish writing them.

Most companies participating in this program make it easy on their managers and supervisors and provide each a supply of 4" x 6" heavy stock cards, blank or with the company's logo, along with matching envelopes.

As you will learn in Chapter 12, when we discuss the interdependence of the tools, blank *Care Cards* are often kept in a designated area that houses all of the materials necessary to make the tools most accessible and easy to use. But regardless where your *Care Cards* are kept, you should have a supply of them handy at all times, along with envelopes and a pen.

(4) "Where Can I Find The Address?"

You shouldn't have to look for an address. Every company has the addresses of their employees, and that information should, in turn, be provided to managers in readily accessible form. In turn, you as a manager should keep that list in a safe place, or on your computer. Microsoft Outlook™, for example, has an excellent searchable address list and you can enter fifty employees and their addresses in less than an hour.

Other companies provide a master employee list in a room designated for managers to use at the beginning and end of each day, solely for the purpose of utilizing the tools, a place where managers and supervisors congregate at the end of their workdays and shifts to write *Care Cards,* update their *Milestone Boxes,* and write in their *Manager's Journals.*

(5) "Who Has A Stamp?"

Every company that has adopted this program provides stamps to supervisors and managers. If your company hasn't caught on, then stock up yourself at your local post office. Get a roll of stamps and keep it handy.

How about your company's postage meter? Like e-mail, don't even think about it. There are not many universal truths when it comes to personal correspondence, but here's one of the big ones: *never use a postage meter to send a personal note.* Why? Look in your own mailbox and the answer will be obvious. Look at the mail that comes with postage meter indicia; almost all junk mail or bills, aren't they? Then look at the mail that comes with a first class stamp with a hand-written address. Rarely junk. We rest our case.

(6) "Where Do I Mail My Care Card?"

A post office would be the obvious place, but no one has time to go the post office anymore; most of us don't even know the location of the post office; and unless we're buying a post office box, there's really no reason to make the trek. If you are reading this book because your company has adopted the Credible Connections program, you will have a tray, bin, or box for outgoing mail; usually in the same area, you will find blank *Care Cards,* stamps, and a mailing list. Finish your *Care Cards,* address them, stamp them, and toss them in the outgoing mail tray.

No card, no address, no postage, no one to mail the card for you? Those objections are history. Do you have any others? Perhaps so. If you're like most managers whom we have trained, you have one substantive objection: "I don't know how to write a card." No problem. We'll get to that before you finish this chapter. But first, let's take a look at the methodology of one electronics company and how *Care Cards* are handled there—that is, how they get a *Care Card* from the manager's hands into the hands of the employee.

Care Card Procedure

> *(1) When a "significant event" occurs in one of your employees' lives, you will find blank cards and envelopes in our "Credible Connections" room. Per your training, these are cards to express your personal sentiments. Please write your note on a card. Place the card in a matching envelope, which you will also find there. You will find the employee's current address on the Master List (which should not be taken for any reason from the "Credible Connections" room). After addressing, place the envelope in the Care Card Outbox. All Care Cards in the Outbox by 5 p.m. each day will be hand-stamped and mailed that day.*

Easy? You bet, and most managers have told us that it takes the "hassle" out of the experience.

(7) "How Do I Write A Care Card?"

Many managers haven't written a personal note in years, if ever. It is not that managers don't have feelings, but only that they have never been taught to write them down, and it's difficult to be good at something you have never done. How did you fare the first time you rode a bicycle, disciplined an employee, or told someone that you loved them? Now that you've done all those things many times, you're better at them, so let's learn how to write a great *Care Card.*

As a general proposition, what you write should be what comes to your head or to your heart after thinking about it for a minute or two. If you learn to listen very carefully, you will hear a small voice whispering amid all that information that is force-fed into your consciousness each day. Those who are not used to writing often don't hear this voice at first over all the noise. It is why personal correspondence, not just *Care Cards,* is always best written in a quiet place, a place where you can quiet your mind and just *feel.* Remember the admonition of James Joyce. "No pen, no ink, no table, no room, no time, no quiet, no inclination."[cxl]

Once you're ready, enter the *Care Card* experience with an open mind and be willing to write whatever comes to your mind. Remember that the purpose of the *Care Card* is to express *your* thoughts and *your* feelings about a person or an event. You are trying to feel what they are feeling. You are trying to perceive, understand, and communicate. So, do it. Put yourself in your employee's position, knowing what you know about him or her, and look around you. What do you see? What do you feel? What are you thinking? What are you happy about? What is making you sad? What are you afraid of? Those thoughts and feelings are the ones about which you want to write.

The Best Technique? Yours, Of Course

Molière observed, "I always write a good first line, but I have trouble writing the others." Interestingly, most of us do not share Molière's challenge. To the contrary, the first line of a note or letter or *Care Card* is almost always the toughest, so here's a tip: just begin. Don't think too long. Don't edit mentally. Don't wait for the perfect sentence. Once you've spent the minute or so thinking about what you want to say, just write. If it turns out your first few tries aren't right or don't express what you want to say or what you feel, no problem. Paper is cheap. Give it another try, two or three, if necessary. Like riding that bicycle, you'll get it, and this experience will be one that won't subject you to bruises.

If you're stuck, begin by saying where you are or what you are doing. That can segue into what you're thinking and feeling. Here's a good example:

> Dear Sam,
>   The parking lot at the plant is wet from the rain right now. It is easy to complain when you are soaking wet by the time you get to your car, but then I think of life's real challenges, such as those you face in your battle with cancer.

While I'm sure you would have chosen another challenge had you been able to choose, this is one you will be proud to have conquered. And you will conquer your illness, just as you have conquered every other challenge I have seen you face, in the workplace and out.

I will be visiting you this weekend and if I get a little wet, so be it. If I hear others complain about the weather or other trivial asides, I'll remember that's no challenge at all. I'll look forward to talking Saturday.

Keep the faith.

/s/ John

For some people, it is difficult to talk about their feelings, but remember that personal correspondence, including *Care Cards,* is about how *you* feel, either about the employee to whom you are writing, or as you see the circumstances they are experiencing through his or her eyes. Either way, to begin with, "I" is not poor form or selfish, and you will find yourself doing it often.

Try to avoid beginning a *Care Card* with an apology for tardiness, and try not to be late in acknowledging an important event. If someone needs to be congratulated, write it while you feel the need to write it and can be sincere and be enthusiastic about the event—always the same day, if possible.

As you can see, there's not too many "thou shalt nots" when it comes to writing *Care Cards.* Here are two examples of *Care Cards* written by managers out of our seminars that illustrate just how easy it is to write one and write it well:

Letter of Congratulations

Dear Bill:

When I saw you walk across the company cafeteria this morning to accept the Employee of the Month award, I just about stood up and cheered! I have seen many in other departments—people I do not know well—receive the award, but you are the first I have worked with who was so honored. You are deserving of this award and we in the Parts Department are very proud of you. I have a feeling that I'll see you reach out and accept that award again, and I'll be just as proud of you that day as I am today.

Thanks!

/s/Jim

Condolences on Death of A Loved One

While notes of congratulations are the easiest and most fun to write, cards of condolence, sadness, and sorrow are the most difficult and serious, yet often the most meaningful. Like all *Care Cards,* they need not be tomes or epistles. Emily Dickenson once described receiving a card after her father's death: "One [writer] who only said 'I am sorry' helped me the most." Oftentimes, the most effective *Care Cards* expressing condolence observe the qualities of the deceased, how you felt about him or her, and even better, how he or she felt about the recipient of the letter, if you know. Here's one *Care Card* written by a manager to the wife of a deceased employee, using what he knew, along with information from his *Milestone Box:*

Dear Jennifer:

I know you have heard the stories about John's generosity. I knew John for five years, and during that time I saw him give his lunch, his coat, and yes, once even his shirt, to a co-worker who had his torn badly by a machine.

While John and I were not life-long friends, I felt a special bond with him. Many people here did. We worked together not only here, but during the holiday seasons at "Meals On Wheels," and I am better for having served our community with him.

John always spoke highly of you. As you must know, he loved you very much, and unlike many men who are too "macho" to talk about things like that, John was always first to say what a wonderful wife he had and how proud he was of her.

Please call me if there is anything I can do.

Respectfully,

Don

Notice that while these two *Care Cards,* one of congratulations and the other of condolence, are very different in substance, they share spontaneity. They just "blurt" it out. The manager put his thoughts together and said what he felt—no more, no less—and in both, he recited important personal facts about the employee. You should do the same, and even though your grammar may not be perfect and you may misspell a word from time to time, your effort will be worthwhile if it expresses your feelings. Abraham Lincoln, after all, was a notoriously bad speller, and he wrote the Gettysburg address, on which history gave him an "A." No one cared about his orthographic failures, and no one will care about yours, either.

While the rules of writing personal notes are few, there are a few caveats worth remembering: First, do not dwell on your own problems and thereby diminish someone else's experience by describing a similar experience of your own. Likewise, do not tell the other person how you would feel or what you would do if you were experiencing their circumstance. That may be sympathetic, but it is not empathetic, and the expression of the empathy is the highest use of *Care Cards.* Finally, do not end your *Care Card* by indicating that you are "busy" or "must run now, the telephone's ringing." Your phone shouldn't be ringing when you are writing a *Care Card,* and you should not diminish the importance of the event about which you are writing by excusing yourself to more important tasks.

Ending Your Care Card

Ending a *Care Card* is difficult for some managers. Most of us, after all, didn't attend charm school and so we don't know whether "Sincerely," "Yours truly," "Best wishes," or one of the other myriad of salutations, is appropriate under any given circumstance. But the end is the like the beginning. Say what you feel. To help you out, here are some basic guidelines:

Formal Salutations (often used for a condolence letter to an employee who has experienced a death in the family): "Respectfully," "Respectfully yours," and "Very truly yours."

Informal Salutations (used for most every other situation): "Cordially," "Sincerely," or "Sincerely yours."

Or, don't use a salutation. Just say what you want to say, stop, and sign your name. That's fine, too.

118

You have written your *Care Card*. What happens next? Good things.

More Rewards: Writer as Reader

Managers generally get what they reward in the workplace. With *Care Cards,* we call it the "reciprocity of kindness." One act of kindness begets another. When managers send *Care Cards,* they almost magically begin receiving cards and notes from their employees. They want to connect, too, and enjoy a quality relationship. In fact, it is not uncommon for employees to be so overwhelmed by receiving a *Care Card* that they write notes of thanks to those who sent them. Here's one example of a card received by a manager:

> *"I got your card today when I got home. I've worked for a lot of companies and many supervisors, but you're the first who has taken the time to say 'thanks' like this. I want you to know how much I appreciate it."*

Still another benefit to the manager who writes *Care Cards* is the connection made to employees' families, because employees often share *Care Cards* with their family members. When you learn that a member of an employee's immediate family has achieved something of moment, especially when you learn of that achievement from the employee himself, write the family member a *Care Card.* After all, they usually live at the same address as the employee, and if they don't, ask the employee. "I know you are proud that your son is graduating from college, Bob. Do you mind if I send Johnny a note of congratulations? What's his address?" Jot it down. When you are updating your *Milestone Box* at the end of the day, write a *Care Card,* too, and tell John just how proud his Dad is of him!

Who Writes The Best Care Cards?

Which managers are best at writing *Care Cards*? Those who *care* the most are almost always the best at expressing that care. Nothing exudes emotion like real emotion. In fact, those who are genuine in their expressions are more effective than those who care less but write better. Affection works; affectation does not.

That said, we have noticed that female managers are usually better at writing *Care Cards* than their male counterparts. There are many psychological explanations for this phenomenon, the most common one of which is that women are more in touch with their emotions, and we are not the only ones to notice this. The English management guru, Charles Handy, observed this quality in female managers:

> *"The feminine strain shows itself not just in the physical presence of more women [in the workplace], but also in a heightened awareness of creativity, sensitivity, personal relationships and feelings, personal worth and individual differences. Men care about these things, too, of course— some of them more than some women do—but a predominately male culture will keep such things under cover and control and will promote toughness, discipline, and impersonality."*[cxli]

In other words, we men, in our effort to be strong, often hide our feelings and emotions. Many of us were taught early that feelings and their expression are for women. Women learned it, too, and that is why they are often more empathetic, enjoy more and better relationships with others, and as a gender, are happier than men.[cxlii]

Others believe women are better at personal correspondence simply because they write more personal correspondence than most men. Regardless of the reason, we find the best teachers of *Care Card* writing to be women and the good news is that those some of those women are in your workplace. Man or woman, if you know someone who is good at writing personal letters, cards, and notes—inside or outside the workplace—talk to them. Take a few lessons. They will be happy to help. Just remember, your teachers and mentors in *Care Card* writing are not there to write your *Care Cards* for you; they are there to help you learn the skill of transferring something in your head or your heart onto paper.

"How Many Care Cards Should I Write?"

How many? That's the most common question we hear, but there is no answer. It depends on how many employees you know and manage, how many opportunities you have, how attentive you are, how much you care, how often you update your *Milestone Box* and *Manager's Journal*, and how many minutes a week you are willing to spend to create relationships with those for whom you are responsible. In some situations, you may write someone for no apparent reason and be like Henry Miller who once observed, "It does me good to write a letter which is not a response to a demand—a gratuitous letter, so to speak, which has accumulated in me like the waters of a reservoir."[cxliii] You will find that the more you write *Care Cards*, the more of them you will want to write.

As a median or average, however, we find successful managers, those with a sincere desire to establish relationships, write an average of 3-5 *Care Cards* per year per employee. If you are a manager who is responsible for 30 employees, that would be a total of 90 to 150 Care Cards a year. That sounds like a lot until you consider that there are approximately 230 working days a year. Even at the high end of the Care Card spectrum, that's less than one *Care Card* per working day.

Where can you find the extra minutes to write? That is up to you, but we recommend taking that extra time out of your television allotment. Since television has been shown to make us less content with what we have and in turn more violent and aggressive, do a favor for yourself and others: write more and watch less.

The New Archetype: The Caring Mentor

Care Cards have become an archetype of many successful managers—managers who are ardent and passionate about mentoring those for whom they have assumed responsibility. While some effort is required, the effort is not arduous, and if you are like the thousands of managers we have worked with, you will soon be a believer once you have given *Care Cards* a try and have seen the results.

That's it. You now have three of the most powerful tools of relationship-based management. This leaves us only to show you how they work together—in tandem—as a powerful combination to create workplace relationships.

CHAPTER 12

Implementing And Using The Tools In Tandem

I began with the Milestone Box, added Care Cards a few months later, and then after six months seeing it all work, I added the Manager's Journal. It was only once I saw how they related to each other in practice, how each is interdependent on the others, that I was able to maximize the effect and become fully effective as a relationship-based manager. I don't want to gloat, but now, after a year, I know each of my employees as individuals. They know me. I understand each is unique, different, and the words "empathy" and "relationship" have new meanings for me and I have a new meaning as a manager and, I believe, as a human being.

- Alice, Receiving Manager, 2002

THE *Milestone Box, Manager's Journal, and Care Cards* can be used independently. Some managers, like Alice, chose to implement one tool first, later adding the other tools as she became comfortable and convinced of their value. Regardless of whether they are implemented serially or together, every manager with whom we have worked finds that the tools are more powerful when used in tandem, that is, when their synergies are understood and exploited. In this chapter we examine these synergies, as well as synergies among managers who use them and how the sum of the parts can, indeed, be greater than the whole in the creation of relationships.

Before examining the tools and their relationships to each other, let's first explore how the tools are best implemented in an institutional setting. What kind of commitment is required of you and of your organization when adopting the relationship paradigm? How have organizations assisted managers in using the program most effectively without wasting time?

Rollout, Training and Implementation

Like most systems and programs, how best to implement the three tools has not been the subject of theory, but rather has been proven via trial, error, and success over several years. What we have learned from our clients may help you.

Training

Most management "systems" and "programs" fail, not because managers were not shown how to do it right or because they are too complicated, but rather because managers never bought in to the program at the outset. Managers often laugh sardonically when we begin our session, wondering whether this will be another "HR program du jour," at first mandated by their company, then fail over time without upper management support, and ultimately be replaced with the next program.

We would be less than honest to represent that Credible Connections and these tools have been successful in every workplace and with every manager. They have not. This is why we regularly turn down companies seeking to implement the program if we are not convinced there is sufficient commitment at the highest levels to relationship-based management and the use of the tools.

Even with that support, to insure success individual managers must accept satisfaction at work as a proper and achievable goal. This requires dialog, because like most employees, many managers come to us with a view that satisfaction and happiness are independent of work, even mutually exclusive in some cases. As one manager told us, "Happy is what you are when you *aren't* at work." Through dialog and training, this manager and many others have changed their minds, but not without accepting the following premises, essential to using the tools effectively:

1. Most employees are not satisfied or happy at work. They would do something else today other than come to their current job if they had a choice.
2. Work for most employees is not inherently "meaningful"—that is, work that provides "inner meaning," work for which they have a genuine passion.
3. Beyond food, shelter, and clothing, money and stuff is not related to long-term happiness.
4. Most companies use more, or at least the appearance of more money and benefits to buy employee happiness, and they have failed.
5. Meaningful relationships are a foundation of long-term happiness.
6. Relationships are built upon empathy.
7. Empathy requires knowledge of the other person in order to "see it the way he sees it."
8. Effective empathy toward an employee requires recollection of significant emotional events, and other milestone events in that employee's life.

9. Overwork and information overload, combined with the number of employees managed, makes tools essential to recollection and implementation of effective empathy.

10. The three tools—*Milestone Box, Manager's Journal,* and *Care Cards*—will assist the relationship-based manager in both recollecting and implementing empathy in the development of meaningful relationships with her employees.

We provide this checklist to each manager at the end of our training program, suggesting that until they agree with all ten that they should *not* implement the tools. This is one system where form cannot be elevated over substance and be successful.

To garner the requisite "buy in" is one reason we wrote this book. Our training sessions are important, useful, enjoyable, and supporting, but in just a day or two we cannot recite, train, and expect recollection of every fact, statistic, study, and anecdote we have recounted here. We view training as important, even essential, but it is not a substitute for reading, studying, and understanding what you have read here. If a manager cannot, or will not take a yellow highlighter in hand and read this book cover to cover, training is a waste of time and money. In short, there is no "Cliff Notes" version, which is why those managers who skip to the last chapter in hopes of finding a convenient summary will be disappointed.

Implementation Order: One, Two, Or All

The question for some managers is whether to implement the tools one at a time or as an integrated package: the suite of tools. We have seen it accomplished successfully both ways, and here are the considerations:

A Foot in the Water—One Tool at a Time

On the theory that jumping off the edge of a swimming pool should come before diving in head first from a three meter board, some companies elect to implement one tool at a time. They do it this way in order to insure a full and complete understanding of each tool before moving to the next one. This usually means implementing the *Milestone Box* first, followed by the *Care Card,* which, as you will see, are very interdependent and only later, the *Manager's Journal*—arguably the most powerful of the tools—but also the most challenging.

Still other employers and managers implement one tool at a time believing, oftentimes correctly, that their managers are overloaded and are best not overwhelmed by implementing what they see as three separate initiatives. Still other employers and managers take the "show me" approach, and implement a second and then a third tool only after the first is proven to be effective.

One at a time makes sense, is logical, and it works. But, the one-step-at-a-time approach ignores an important fact: the tools, while they appear to be separate and have been discussed individually, are integrally related and interdependent. While they can be used individually, just as a hammer can be used separately from a saw, they are best used together if your goal is to build a house.

Diving In Headfirst—Use of the Tools as a Suite

Learning the tools one at a time, using them, and then integrating them adds a step in the process, and we have found that managers who have learned the tools individually tend to continue to view them that way and have a more significant challenge when they integrate them later.

Use of the tools is much like swimming—comprising several components—kicking with the feet, crawling with the arms, and turning the head into and out of the water to breathe. While we do not advocate dumping managers into deep water if they have never learned how to swim, neither do we believe that continuing to practice the individual elements of swimming is the best way to learn to swim. Rather, once the foundation is built—that is, the belief system about work, what it can provide us and what it cannot, and the technical requirements of the tools are understood—we encourage managers to actually swim, in the shallow water at first, which encourages an early integration of purpose, function, and utility. Managers kick, crawl and breathe at the same time, swimming slowly at first, but soon getting the hang of it and moving farther and faster.

Most organizations that implement the tools as a suite set modest initial goals for managers, such as one *Care Card*, two *Milestone Cards*, and three entries into their *Manager's Journal* each week for the first few weeks, followed by a Roundtable (discussed later in this chapter) to provide input and critique. The bar may be raised another time or two, but oftentimes this is not necessary. Soon managers are swimming, some better than others, but each understanding how to swim and taking responsibility for improving their strokes.

As with any task, some managers are naturally better than others. Some will swim end-to-end in the pool the second week after they learn how to swim. Others take it slower. Regardless, managers who combine their beliefs and understanding with use of the tools and make the minimal time commitment necessary to be effective get good results over time, swimming farther and faster each time they dive in.

Time Commitment

"How much time is this going to take?"

This is the question most often asked by managers during training. Use of time for any purpose precludes its use for any other purpose, and harried managers understand this physical principle at a cellular level. Their focus on the time that will be sacrificed, rather than the results being achieved, this is the plight of the overworked, overinformationed manager. They cannot create one additional minute in any day. Rather, managers must find the time to use the program by giving up something else they are doing, or by doing it more efficiently.

Most managers overestimate the amount of time they will need to spend utilizing the tools, and they underestimate the time they will spend listening and learning from their employees. Assuming that the logistics of "where" and "when" are thought through and a system has been developed, we find most managers spend an average of fifteen minutes a day actually writing. How much time they spend discovering the events to document varies by how effective they are listening, the number of employees they manage, and their current relationships with existing employees.

Where and When: The "Credible Connections Room"

The manager's time commitment is also dependent upon the commitment of his company. If his organization has rolled out initiative after initiative, supported them briefly, only to kill them off or let them fail, managers will be initially resistant and stand back to determine whether this program really has the backing and commitment of the organization. This slows development.

How best to communicate "real commitment" depends upon the culture of the organization, but tying the success of the manager to the success of the manager's use of the tools, making it an integral part of evaluating his performance, has proven effective. "You're doing well, Bob, but your *Milestone Box* reflects no attempt to create relationships." This often results in undivided attention of a manager and helps him understand the program's importance to the company; at least the system pays dividends to the individual manager, after which no further prodding is necessary.

Likewise, logistical assistance rendered by the organization enhances managerial commitment to the program by minimizing the time tradeoff experienced by managers. Many companies, for example, set up a *Credible Connections Room* to which managers go to write each day. In this clean, secure, well-lighted place are tables, chairs, and a locking file cabinet in which managers store their *Milestone Boxes* and *Manager's Journals*. There is a plentiful stock of blank *Care Cards, Milestone Cards*, notebook paper, pens, stamps, employee rosters with addresses, and often a photocopier.

One device notably missing from the *Credible Connections Room* is a telephone. Its absence is intentional, because when a manager arrives there at the end of his workday, he is not present to transact business as usual. To the contrary, he is there to put busyness behind him, to sit, think, and reflect upon the day's events, to separate the important from the unimportant, and to document the former by *Care Card, Milestone Card*, and *Manager's Journal*. At the end of the week, the *Credible Connections Room* is a place managers can take time to review their efforts, including a review of their *Manager's Journals*.

The Tools in Tandem

While logistics like stamps, mailing services, and supplies are important and conducive to managerial commitment, in the end it is what managers know, remember, document, and follow up on that lead to relationships and effective relationship-based management. Using the tools most effectively means understanding their relationships and their synergies.

Milestone Box: The Relationships and Synergies With Care Cards and the Manager's Journal

The *Milestone Box* documents the most significant and memorable events in the lives of your employees. Many milestone events, as we have noted, are appropriately acknowledged by *Care Card*, just as other milestone events become topics of discussion in the *Manager's Journal*. For example, if the wife of one your employee's gives birth, it is appropriate to document that fact in the *Milestone Box* for later follow-up. From the *Milestone Card* you will write a *Care Card* and send it to the employee, acknowledging the event and expressing congratulations, but if the employee distills that event into a belief—"I don't believe we can afford another child"—it should also be documented in the *Manager's Journal*. It may become the topic of a discussion about money and budgeting later.

Milestone Box as a Care Card Reminder

Milestone events are often the subject of *Care Cards*; birthdays, anniversaries, births and deaths in an employee's family are good examples of milestone events generally appropriate for *Care Cards*. But how does a manager remember all of these important events over time? The answer, as we have seen, is the *Milestone Box,* and many managers get double-duty by using their *Milestone Box* as a tickler system to send *Care Cards*. For example, when an employee's birthday is recorded in the *Milestone Box*, the manager has a reminder to send a *Care Card* annually to mark the event. To do this effectively requires the manager to stay a week or two ahead in the review of his *Milestone Box*, checking important dates into the future. By so doing, *Care Cards* are written and mailed in time to insure delivery on or before the event to be acknowledged.

Milestone Box As a Cross-Reference to the Manager's Journal

Milestone events such as the death of a family member or close personal friend trigger the creation of a milestone card for purposes of manager follow-up, but due to the intensity and meaning of these significant emotional experiences, such events often result in discussion, observation, and distillation by the employee. In the case of a death in the family, for example, an employee may lament the times that could have been spent with the loved one but were not. Still others resolve to live life differently after the death of a significant other. Such lamentations, resolutions, and other expressions and distillations should be recorded in the *Manager's Journal* to help the manager see the event through the eyes of his employee, the *sine qua non* of empathetic response, and may be useful in helping the employee with other life challenges later.

Both entries are important, but your ability to understand the event will be enhanced if the *Milestone Card* is cross-referenced with your *Manager's Journal* so when the *Milestone Card* comes to your attention, you are reminded to review the earlier entry in your *Manager's Journal* that ties the milestone event to the results, thoughts, feelings, and beliefs that were expressed by the employee about the event. By making a simple notation on the *Milestone*

Card, to-wit, that a *Manager's Journal* entry was made and the day it was made, the later acknowledgement of the event by *Care Card*, for example, will be more than generic, but will include a meaningful recollection observation of the life lost and recount employee lessons learned based on the reflections of the employee.

Care Cards: The Relationships and Synergies With the Milestone Box and the Manager's Journal

Although *Care Cards* often are created from events recorded in a manager's *Milestone Box* or from expressions recorded in the *Manager's Journal*, most often they are created in real time upon learning of an important event in an employee's life. The *Milestone Box* and *Manager's Journal* entries, if any, are created from the *Care Card*.

The Milestone Card Created From the Care Card

Certain events that *Care Cards* acknowledge, *e.g.*, births, deaths, anniversaries, and the like, are also milestone events. The careful manager, upon sending a *Care Card*, will make a determination as to whether or not the event being acknowledged is a milestone event upon which he wants to follow up in the future. If so, a *Milestone Card* should be created, along with the *Care Card*, and filed in the *Milestone Box* to include an entry on the *Milestone Card* that a *Care Card* was sent to the employee on that date.

The Manager's Journal as a Repository for Care Cards

Care Cards, as we learned, palpably express the sentiments of a manager to an employee after, or in anticipation of a significant event. The *Manager's Journal*, as a repository for the sentiments, beliefs, and distillations of experiences expressed by employees, is the perfect place to keep photocopies of *Care Cards* that were sent. In fact, for some managers, each *Care Card* acts as an independent entry into their *Manager's Journal*, thus reminding the manager of his own thoughts, beliefs, and feelings at the time he expressed those sentiments in writing. The ability to remember what you wrote will be helpful to your meaningful reflection of events months or years into the future.

Manager's Journal: The Relationships and Synergies With the Milestone Box and Care Cards

While some milestone events are shared by all employees, such as birthdays and employment anniversaries, certain other events are unique to individual employees. A good example was Mary's cat. Mary worked for Joe, an alert manager who knew that Mary had lost her husband fourteen years before, and that Suzy, her cat, had been her only full-time companion since that tragedy in her life. He knew the affection Mary felt toward Suzy, that

127

the animal was more like a child to her than a pet, and there were several *Manager's Journal* entries over the years attesting to that fact. The loss of Suzy was a milestone in Mary's life, making her different from another employee whose loss of a pet might be hurtful, but not a milestone event. In Mary's situation, Joe properly recorded the event in his *Manager's Journal*. Might a *Milestone Box* entry be appropriate under these circumstances? Yes. How about a *Care Card*? Yes, once again, and the *Manager's Journal* entry was the trigger for both.

Unique Milestones Mined in the Manager's Journal

Mary's alert and caring manager recognized that the death of Mary's pet was a milestone event in her life. Joe created a *Milestone Card* and followed up appropriately. On the *Milestone Card*, in addition to the date and brief description of the event, was a notation that a *Manager's Journal* entry had been made, thus returning Joe, Mary's manager, to the time and place and her feelings at such a time that in the future it becomes appropriate or helpful to recall them in service to Mary.

Care Card Opportunities in the Manager's Journal

In most cases, a *Care Card* would not be written to an employee upon losing a pet. However, as we noted, the differences in feelings among different employees to different events requires different responses. Mary appreciated the *Care Card* sent by her manager that acknowledged her feelings and her individuality. Mining this opportunity from his *Manager's Journal* entry brought Mary and her manager closer together.

Synergy Among Managers: The Roundtable

The synergies of the tools—*Care Cards, Milestone Box,* and *Manager's Journal*—act to make their combined effect greater than the sum of their individual values. There is another synergy that is equally important: cooperative interaction among managers who are participating in the Credible Connections program. This synergy emanates from their regular sharing of ideas, methods, and problems, both substantive and logistic.

Harkening back to our comments about training, once the program is understood no learning is better than peer learning—a continuing experience. After a modicum of success in using the program, we find that managers are most anxious to learn more about how to use it and crave input from others, especially their peers who are likewise using the tools.

Bringing managers together regularly in roundtable discussions permits them to share successes and learn from mistakes, both their own and others'. Setting ground rules only with regard to confidentiality (managers must remember that the *Manager's Journal*, in particular, contains that which should be presumed to be confidential) open discussions of substantive workplace issues; often endemic issues and problems are highly effective. We find endemic issues are often replete in *Manager's Journals*. From complaints about wages, to benefits, to impediments, to getting the job done, to management style, to leadership, to quirks of individual managers—there is always plenty to discuss and work through at a manager's Roundtable.

For example, a manager reviewing his *Manager's Journal* may see that many of his employees believe the facility manager to be detached, aloof, and use as evidence his regular absence from the plant floor. Without comparing notes, so to speak, this manager cannot be sure whether the problem goes beyond his department and his employees or whether this problem is shared by employees plant-wide. This manager quickly learns the answer to that question when he tosses the subject onto the Roundtable for discussion. Parenthetically, such a topic is more likely to be made the subject of discussion where mid-managers, otherwise fearful of bringing criticisms of senior management individually, find strength in numbers.

How often should Roundtables be scheduled? This is much like the question "How many *Care Cards* should I write?" The more the better, but they should be held at least quarterly. The closer Roundtables are to the events discussed by the managers attending, the more likely they are to be understood and resolved. If there is a particular operations or policy change that gives rise to concern or complaint, they can be dealt with early in their development.

Finally, there are individual employee issues that, while they must be handled confidentially, can often be handled effectively via hypothetical questions to the group. "If you had an employee who came to you and admitted the abuse of prescription drugs, how would you handle it? What are the options?" Without revealing the employee's identity, others who comprise the Roundtable can lend their expertise to particular employee challenges, including their own experiences and knowledge of help available outside the organization, and as a byproduct they can keep the organization away from allegations of discrimination, alleging that one manager handled the problem differently than another.

Taking part in Roundtables should be all managers who are actively using the tools, and thereby have something to learn and to share. Also effective in Roundtables can be in-house experts on issues such as law, ethics, safety, and human resources, but we have found the "pros" are often best involved *after* the discussion of issues among participating management peers. In that way, the expertise and power of the professionals is not unduly restrictive or intimidating to the managers who are sharing and learning.

Another caveat regarding use of in-house experts is that some have a propensity to get to "no" instead of getting to "yes." Many lawyers, for example, often look at any writing—even something as simple and straightforward as a *Care Card*—not for its intended purpose, but for its evidentiary possibilities. Human resources personnel, too, are sometimes an impediment in Roundtables, viewing all corporate humanity as their "turf" and this system as a diminution of their power. In the worst cases, when in-house legal counsel and the human resources department combine forces in an effort to kill an initiative, the result can be devastating. More companies need to recall that in-house experts exist to provide necessary, yet ancillary, services to the management of any organization, and more of these staffers need to understand business does not revolve around their narrow function, but the other way around. This understanding is of particular importance to the success of this program, where relationships are embraced rather than shunned and a non-traditional paradigm of work is embraced. We have found that theoretical boogie-men lurk in the minds of those who understand too much about too little. A morbid imagination, combined with superior knowledge in a single area can result in a dozen reasons why not to lend aid to a fellow human being. This is not to say that the experts should not have a say. They should, but with the directive that they are to figure out how to make the system work within the confines of their specialty, not merely to provide 100 theoretical reasons why it won't work.

Synergy: Different Strokes for Different Folks

How the program is introduced and implemented is unique to each organization. Thus each tool, both individually and as a system, must be adapted to unique work environments. That is one reason why in our training sessions we open it up for discussion, outlining the basics and seeking the input and ultimate buy-in of the supervisors who will be utilizing the tools and working out a plan of action with them.

Size of the company, facilities, culture, commitment of upper management, sophistication of line management and availability of supporting staff functions are but a few of the many factors that should be weighed in order to design the program to insure its success, but these considerations, individually and collectively, pale in importance to the commitment of individual managers to the goal: employee satisfaction through meaningful relationships. Until a manager views this as a fundamental directive, not necessarily one commanded by an organization, but as the *sine qua non* of living a good life, there will be no break-throughs. For some, this only occurs after going through the motions, with the program becoming effective for some managers via modification of behavior over time. However it happens, it happens, and it happens in a different way within every corporation and within every manager.

Impact Upon Employees

For employees, the system provides the rewards we have discussed. They often comment after not too many months that they have a "new manager," one with the same face but with new abilities to recall not only the most important events in their lives, but one who makes use of their beliefs and opinions on the important issues of life. Employees will likewise notice the physical changes, such as cards in their mailboxes. Most will accept these changes with open arms, never looking a gift horse in the mouth.

Others, however, will ask, "Why? Why do you suddenly act like you care about me as a person?" Ironically, some managers have a problem with the answer to this question, as if the tools we have outlined are some sort of sleight-of-hand trick that must be explained away or even denied. The best answer to this question—the only answer, once again—is this truth: "I care enough about you to want to get to know you better. I'll do the best I can as we go along getting to know each other, and I would like your input. I want you to tell me if I am being helpful to you as a resource, both professionally and personally. I want to know if I am being successful in trying to build a stronger relationship between us."

Accepted or questioned, as managers utilize the tools and create and nurture stronger relationships, it is their own creativity that fully synergizes the program. Everyone takes away new and better ideas and methods to connect and create the all-important relationships that are the progenitors of workplace satisfaction and happiness.

PART V

Conclusion

Where Do We Go From Here?

CHAPTER 13

Relationships At A Crossroads In The Future
Of The American Workplace

We have used the tools for a year. You told us that it would make our workplace a better place and it has done that. What you did not tell us is that the tools would change us, make us better managers, and more importantly—more compassionate people, and that, to me, and has been the real victory here, personally and professionally.

- Carl, Vice President Industrial Relations

IN the final chapter of many business books, the authors dutifully summarize the content, outlining the problems they have set out to solve, their premises for resolution, and their optimistic projections for the future. The danger in so doing is providing readers an opportunity to skip the detail and get to the "bottom line." In some texts, there is no harm done. In others, the magic *is* the detail. Such is the case here.

So if you have jumped ahead to this final chapter in an effort to save time and mine whatever nuggets of wisdom may be contained between these covers, you will not find them here. Rather, what useful information exists will be left strewn throughout the text. The tools best serve those who adopt the foundations upon which they rest, to include an understanding of why work isn't working anymore.

This means examining our work and the work of others, what it means, and why. It requires understanding the *Myths of Work* that gets most employees to their jobs each day but has not satisfied them. It means being open to the possibility that the source of satisfaction in the workplace is some place other than where most business organizations and managers have been looking. It means reflecting on our own lives, relationships, and valuing our own experiences, to include our positive relationships with others, and how they contribute to our personal satisfaction. It means recognizing that none of us is independent, that we have dependent needs that can only be satisfied by others— both inside and outside the workplace. Only after having gone through these thought processes do the tools make sense, tools that were not developed by us from whole cloth or even simultaneously. Personal correspondence, reminder systems, and diaries all predated us by many centuries. Rather, we merely borrowed and adapted these tools for the workplace and connected them after seeing a need for busy managers to develop relationships essential to workplace satisfaction and contentment.

Now, a few years later, as we observe the success of the tools, we do not strike the noble pose and predict a radical paradigm shift within most business organizations from one of animated greed to one of human compassion. Rather, we agree with R. H. Tawney who observed that "... no change of system or machinery can avert those causes of social malaise which consist in the egotism, greed, or quarrelsomeness of human nature. What it can do is to create an environment in which those are not the qualities which are encouraged."[cxlv] The tools serve this purpose: not to change us, but to create an environment in which our virtues are encouraged. In so doing, managers must strike a balance between serving the corporation and serving the humanity for whom they are responsible. The best of business organizations assist them in this effort.

The tools, even if used effectively, will not make the workplace pleasant for everyone who enters there. The tools will not solve problems of unemployment, underemployment, nor will they halt the bulimic hiring and layoff binges most companies now engage in with impunity. The tools will not resolve gross income disparities between Achievers and Survivors, nor will it narrow the income gap between the sexes or races.[cxlvi] The tools do not "reengineer" the American workplace, the prevalent, yet unfulfilled, promise of each successive system of modern management. The endemic conflicts of interest between management and labor await structural resolution to avoid entropy, as does our entire economic system, which is focused solely on producing profit and luxury while ignoring the social and environmental implications of doing so.

The *Milestone Box*, *Manager's Journal*, and *Care Cards*, when used by managers who are open to a different way of thinking, simply make the workplace experience more palatable, enjoyable, compassionate, ethical, joyful, and satisfactory through the creation of meaningful workplace relationships. The best we can hope for is that using the tools will result in managers acting as if people mattered, and then coming to the realization that they *do* matter. Relationship-based managers discover that they have "meaningful work" after all, that their work reflects who they are, and provides "inner meaning" through the expression of care and compassion to others.

From a condition of compassion, more significant changes may be spawned as relationship-based managers take their personal contentment and liberal virtues with them to the tops of organizations to resolve problems through empathy and understanding, rather than worsening them through selfishness and aggression.

Hopes expressed, we are not Pollyannaish about the immediate future. Some people in corporate America will not find this book to be good news. For some seated in the executive suite, we may tug a bit too hard on the curtain that disguises the wizard, making it more difficult to tidy up history by refusing to put a smile on the face of greed. We understand that corporate man serves one master—the organization, and that if relationships become a hurdle to productivity, productivity will win most of the bouts. Fortunately, we have yet to see a workplace that suffered productivity losses after this system was adopted. To the contrary, productivity has risen in those companies who have adopted relationship-based management, if only because satisfied employees are more productive employees.

A few have criticized the tools as "manipulative," finding their use not supported by "genuine empathy." We counter that good deeds often come before, not after, the belief systems that support them, and we agree with Eric Hoffer who once observed, "It is futile to judge a kind deed by its motives. Kindness can become its own motive. We are made kind by being kind."[cxlvii] That has been our experience in the workplace—that modification of behavior is more effective in making real change than selling management theories to overworked,

135

overinformationed managers. We have found that modifying behavior can bring our best nature to the surface through our illustration of compassion, patience, and forgiveness. As a natural consequence of our understanding, we can eliminate, or at least sublimate our anger, jealousy and hatred. And so it has been with most managers with whom we have worked. They are decent people who, consciously or not, chose their profession because they liked other people. The tools simply help caring managers express who they are and what they believe.

Success has bred success. Compassionate, caring relationships among managers and the employees they supervise have increased human satisfaction in many workplaces, and that is a worthwhile goal, is it not?

FOR FURTHER INFORMATION

Jim Karger is a labor lawyer and employee relations consultant with more than 25 years experience counseling employers in the American workplace. Featured in the *Wall Street Journal, Business Week,* and many other publications, Karger is touted as being one of today's best at understanding the psyche and motivation of the American employee. He is available as a keynote speaker and seminar presenter in the areas of the American workplace and employee relations at: karger@crediblyconnect.com.

For more information about the *Credible Connections* program, management training, corporate talks, activities, and other opportunities to "credibly connect" in your workplace, go to www.crediblyconnect.com or call 214-432-5701.

For more information about this book, ordering, and quantity discounts go to www.jimkarger.com.

ENDNOTES

i   In 2002, the Conference Board found only 51 percent of employees satisfied with their jobs, compared with 59 percent in 1995. Tellingly, the most satisfied age groups were those under 25 and over 65, one group that has not spent much time in the workplace and the other knowing they will be leaving soon. The largest decline in overall job satisfaction (60.9 percent in 1995 to 47.2 percent in 2003) occurred among those ages 35-44, once the group most satisfied with work. The second largest decline in job satisfaction was among employees those ages 45-54, their satisfaction dropping from 57.3 percent to 46.1 percent. Even these numbers may underestimate the level of job dissatisfaction because there is evidence that during difficult economic times, when layoffs are prevalent or anticipated, employees respond more positively to such surveys. A good example is the Scripps Howard Data Center survey taken in Texas from August 9 to August 28, 2001, after the slowing economy had driven the State's unemployment rate to 4.7 percent from 4.1 percent in a single month. The survey showed 63 percent of employees felt "very satisfied" with their jobs, up from just 51 percent in 1998. Even the survey's sponsor admitted, "These are people who have survived the layoff for the most part. A lot of people are happy to have a job at this point." *"On The Job And Liking It,"* The Dallas Morning News, September 9, 2001, p. 1H.

ii   Other studies confirm the precipitous decline in employee satisfaction, to include a 2002 Towers Perrin survey, wherein more than 55 percent of workers questioned expressed overall negative feelings about their work. Only 23 percent of respondents said their emotions toward work were "intensely positive."

iii   *Special Consumer Survey Report: Job Satisfaction,* The Conference Board – September 2003, Executive Action Report #68, wherein the overall level of satisfaction among householders earning in excess of $50,000 has declined from 66.5 percent to 53.4 percent. *Also see,* Koretz, G., Yyes, *Workers Are Grumpier – Job Satisfaction Is Falling Sharply,"* Business Week (McGraw-Hill, Inc.), November 13, 2000, p. 42.

iv   Kiplinger's, May, 2001.

v   "Depression is increasingly the reason stated by employees requesting leaves of absence, disability benefits, job changes and reasonable accommodations. There are nearly twice as many employees stating 'depression' as their primary diagnosis [by physicians] for 2001 as in 1999," according to Roslyn Stone, COO of Corporate Wellness Inc., a national occupational health service provider, as cited by Tyler, Kathryn, "Happiness In A Bottle,"

HR Magazine, May, 2002. It is thus not surprising that more than eight in 10 workers plan to look for a new job when the economy heats up, according to a survey by the Society for Human Resource Professionals, cited by *Leslie Haggin Geary, CNN/Money Staff Writer,* in "I Quit! – Overworked employees are fed up: a survey finds 8 out of 10 Americans want a new job," December 30, 2003.

vi   Zelinski, E., "The Joy Of Not Working," (Berkeley, CA.: Ten Speed Press) 1997, p. 72, citing Roper Poll commissioned by *The Wall Street Journal.*

vii   "From vacation homes to cars, consumers are intent on living well. More people consider possessions essential to the good life than did so during the boom times of the late 1990s, according to a RoperASW survey that's tracked consumers' definition of the good life since 1975. Consumers "continue to want it all. Even if they get knocked down a rung, they'll look to get back up as soon as possible." Fifty-two percent of Americans say a second car is essential to the good life, up from 43 percent in 1999, the heyday of the economic boom, according to a survey conducted in February, 2003. Forty-eight percent said a "vacation home" would be necessary, up from 35 percent four years earlier. Even traveling abroad, despite international turmoil, gained stature in consumers' eyes between 1999 and 2003, with 47 percent of consumers considering overseas travel integral to a full life now, up from 37 percent. Owning a home continues its reign at the top of the list, with 89 percent saying it's a necessary part of the good life." Coombes, Andrea, *"Americans Aspiring to and Relating to the Good Life,"* CBSMarketWatch.com, July 25, 2003.

viii   Economic Policy Institute, "Hardships In America: The Real Story of Working Families," July, 2001.

ix   About 47 percent of all babies born in the United States each year participate in the federal Special Supplemental Nutrition Program for Women, Infants and Children, which helps feed 7.7 million people each month by providing vouchers for infant formula, juice, eggs, milk, cheese, cereal and dried beans. See Pear, Robert, "Selling to Poor, Stores Bill U.S. for Top Prices," New York Times, June 6, 2004.

x   Schwartz, Barry, "Tyranny of Choice," Scientific American, April, 2004.

xi   "Office Space," a film by Mike Judge, 20th Century Fox, 1999.

xii   Seligman, Martin E.P., "Authentic Happiness: Using the New Positive Psychology to Realize Your Potential for Lasting Fulfillment," New York: The Free Press, 2002. "In sum, three things reliably predict a heightened sense of gratification and fulfillment for adults: 1) being in a romantic relationship that we consider stable; 2) *being able to perceive how we make a living as a vocation or a calling rather than simply as a job or work;* 3) believing in something larger, or higher, than ourselves. Conversely, there is no significant correlation between wealth, or health, or education, and authentic happiness." Review by Paul Monaco, MSU-Bozeman. *(Emphasis supplied.)*

xiii   The U.S. Department of Labor estimates about 500,000 employees will lose close to 1.2 million workdays due to violence, and lost wages cost employers more than $55 million each year.

xiv   It has been estimated that "most work – 75 percent or more of the tasks in industrial society – are simple and repetitive in nature and for that reason tedious and laborious." Rifkin, Jeremy, "The Age Of Access," Tarcher/Putnam 2000, p. 261.

xv   While the actual number of hours Americans watch TV has been subject to debate, most agree that the number of hours the average American spends in front of the television is between 5.5 and 7 hours per day. See Nielsen Media Research News (New York: A.C.

Nielsen Company, 1990). *Also see* The Kaiser Family Foundation study which reported in 1999 that the hours spent in front of the TV for American children now totals 5 hours and thirty minutes, seven days a week. *Also see* Hepburn, Mary, "The power of the electronic media in the socialization of young Americans; implicator for social studies education," The Social Studies, March 13, 1998, wherein she concludes that television has become the main source of entertainment in America with more than 99 percent of households having at least one television set, two-thirds having two or more, and 54 percent of children having a television set in their bedrooms. The average weekly viewing time has increased since the 1970's to 7 hours per day with children spending an average of 28 hours a week watching television. According to the Henry J. Kaiser Family Foundation's "Kids and Media The New Millennium," which in 1999 surveyed 3,155 children nationally between the ages of 2 and 18, about 65 percent of children ages 8 and older have a TV set in their bedroom, as do 32 percent of children in the 2 to 7 age range. Two-thirds of children reported that they watch television during mealtimes and about the same number said their parents have no set rules about TV watching.

xvi Since 1970, the size of the average house has increased nearly 40%, from about 1,500 square feet to 2,300 square feet in 2002, according to Gopal Ahluwalia, director of research for the National Association of Home Builders, and that is despite an overall decline in family size. From 750 square foot apartments to 2,000 square foot homes to 5,000 square foot estates, where does it end? It doesn't. Look around. If you live in a metropolitan area, you probably know of homes that exceed 20,000 square feet, the size of a full floor in a downtown skyscraper.

xvii 51 percent of American employees surveyed by Roper said that living in a house worth $500,000 or more is evidence of "success," not "excess." Fast Company/Roper Starch Poll, *"How Much Is Enough?,"* Fast Company, July/August, 1999. Interestingly, the same poll found that owning a vacation home, flying the family to Vail yearly to ski, going overseas every year for vacation, driving a BMW or Lexus, having a home theater also were "fruits of success," not "signs of excess." On the other hand, for reasons difficult to fathom, the same employees found paying someone to do all housework, eating a fine restaurant several nights a week, having full-time live-in child care, owning cell-phones for both parents and children, and spending $2,000 on clothes in one day to be "excess," not "success." A comparison of the costs of those luxuries deemed "success," on the whole and individually, arguably exceed those expenses deemed "excessive."

xviii Campbell, Angus, "The Sense Of Well-Being In America," New York, McGraw-Hill, 1981.

xix Elias, Marilyn. "Looks Are a Plus, but Cash Is the King of Hearts," Ithaca Journal, August 19, 1997:B1.

xx See Lane, Robert, "The Loss Of Happiness In Market Democracies," (Yale University Press, 2000), concluding, "Once people rise above the poverty level, there is absolutely no correlation between money and happiness . . . in prosperous countries like the United States, studies have routinely shown that the things that make people happy are family satisfaction, friendships and relationships with other people, but not money." *Also see* Kluwer Academic, "The Journal of Happiness Studies," edited by sociology professor Ruut Veenhoven of Erasmus University Rotterdam who makes a number of counter-intuitive findings, among them: "Above the poverty level, more money does not add much to happiness." Also see Frank, Robert, "Luxury Fever," Princeton University

Press, 1999, wherein he observes"one of the central findings in the large scientific literature on subjective well-being is that once income levels surpass a minimal absolute threshold, average satisfaction levels within a given country tend to be highly stable over time, even in the face of significant economic growth." p. 72.

xxi   Diener, Ed, Journal of Psychological Science, May, 1996.

xxii   *Id.*

xxiii   Lykken, D., "Happiness," St. Martin's Press (New York) 1999, p. 17, citing D.G. Myers and E. Diener, "Who Is Happy?," Psychological Science 6 (1995), p. 10-19.

xxiv   *Id.*

xxv   "People who win the lottery typically report the anticipated rush of euphoria in the weeks after their good fortune. Follow-up studies done after several years, however indicate that these people are often no happier – and indeed, are in some ways less happy – than before." Frank, Robert, "Luxury Fever," Princeton University Press, 1999, p. 76, citing Brickman, P., D. Coates; and R. Janoff-Bulman. "Lottery Winners and Accident Victims: Is Happiness Relative?" Journal of Personality and Social Psychology 36, August 1978; 917-27.

xxvi   Inglehart, "Culture Shift In Advanced Industrial Society," (Princeton University Press, 1990). Also see Frank, Robert, "Luxury Fever," Princeton University Press, 1999, p. 76, citing Brickman, P., D. Coates; and R. Janoff-Bulman. "Lottery Winners and Accident Victims: Is Happiness Relative?" Journal of Personality and Social Psychology 36, August 1978; 917-27, *supra.*

xxvii   See Deiner, Ed, *supra.*

xxviii "Lottery Winners and Accident Victims: Is Happiness Relative?" Journal of Personality and Social Psychology 35 (1978): 917-27; and Argyle, Michael, "The Psychology of Happiness" (London: Methuen, 1986).

xxix   *Id.* "Happiness denotes a subjective appreciation of life by an individual. So there is no given 'objective' standard for happiness. While a person who thinks he has a heart condition may or may not have one, a person who thinks he is happy really is happy." Veenhoven, Ruut, "Correlates of happiness : 7838 findings from 603 studies in 69 nations, 1991-1994," Chapter 2, Erasmus University Rotterdam (1994).

xxx   Some experts on the measurement of happiness contend that only overall happiness can be successfully measured, and that "first asking separate question satisfaction with various domains of life such as 'work', 'marriage' and 'leisure' and next combine the responses in a sum-score . . . has several drawbacks: Firstly, it does not adequately reflect the individuals 'overall evaluation': such sum-scores tap selected aspects of life only, and it is the investigator who awards weights rather than the subject. Secondly, not all aspect-satisfactions apply equally much to everybody; how about the marriage-satisfaction of the unmarried and the job-satisfaction of the unemployed? Thirdly, the significance of life-aspects such as 'work' and 'marriage' is not the same across time, culture and social categories." We take no position on this observation except to observe the obvious – how happy one is with their "work" or "job" clearly has an impact on their overall subjective happiness quotient. It is thus not surprising that overall happiness scores fall on an individual basis when individual factors such as happiness with "work" are low. Veenhoven, Ruut, *supra.*

xxxi   Lykken, D., "Happiness – The Nature and Nurture Of Joy and Contentment (New York: St. Martin's Press) 1999, p. 21.

xxxii   *Id.* at p. 22.

xxxiii Schorr, J., "Overworked American: The Unexpected Decline of Liesure," Basic Books, Reprint Edition, (1993), p. 9

xxxiv More Americans than ever believe that being "very well of financially" is important to their happiness. Between 1967 and 1990, the number of Americans entering college who thought that it was essential to be "very well off financially" rose from 44 percent to 74 percent, according to a study by Eileen M. Crimmins and Richard A. Easterlin. Those who believed it was essential to develop "a meaningful philosophy of life" dropped from 83 percent to 43 percent.

xxxv Fromm, Erich, "The Sane Society," Ch. 5, "Alienation," Henry Holt & Company, Inc.; Reissue edition (October 15, 1990).

xxxvi Handy, Charles, "Gods Of Management: Changing Work of Organizations," Oxford University Pr on Demand; Reprint edition (November 1996), p. 151.

xxxvii "The subjective well-being levels of identical twins reared apart are far more strongly correlated with each other than are the corresponding levels for fraternal twins reared together." Tellegen, Auke, et. al., "Personality Similarity in Twins Reared Apart and Together," Journal of Personality and Social Psychology 54, 1988: 1031-39. *Also see* Lykken, D., "Happiness," St. Martin's Press (new York) 1999, p. 17, citing D.G. Myers and E. Diener, "Who Is Happy," Psychological Science 6 (1995), p. 58.

xxxviii Lykken, D., "Happiness – The Nature and Nurture Of Joy and Contentment," (New York: St. Martin's Press) 1999, p. 3.

xxxix *Id.* at p. 17, citing 1995 studies by David Myers and Ed Diener.

xl A survey of "800 college graduates found that subjects whose values emphasized high income and occupational prestige were twice as likely as others to describe themselves as "fairly unhappy" or "very unhappy." Frank, Robert, "Luxury Fever," Princeton University Press (1999), p. 87, citing Perkins, H.W. "Religious Commitment, Yuppie Values, and Well-Being in Post-Collegiate Life," Review of Religious Research, 32, 1991: 244-51.

xli His Holiness The Dalai Lama and Cutler, Howard, "The Art of Happiness at Work," Riverbend Books (New York), 2003, p. 30. The Dalai Lama argues that the happiest are those who are "freed from the unrealistic expectations about what wealth will provide." *Id.* at p. 62.

xlii Miller, Geoffrey, "Social Policy Implications of the New Happiness Research," http://www.edge.org/3rd_cultur/story/86.html.

xliii Thompson, R., "As Ebenezer Scrooge, Pat Irelan jokes with Rich Leever...", Cincinnati Enquirer, December 9, 1998.

xliv Conlin, Michelle, "The Biggest Wake-Up Call Of My Life," BusinessWeek, October 22, 2001, p. 130.

xlv *Id.* at p. 130.

xlvi Background information and quotes excerpted from the Dallas Morning News, August 27, 2000, "Todd Wagner: Using dot.com wealth to bridge the digital divide," by Lori Stahl.

xlvii Coombes, Andrea, "Study finds workplace values differ between women, men," CBS MarketWatch, June 18, 2004, where a survey of 1,100 workers found that "women are more interested in relationships and recognition at work, while men say pay and achievement are their top priorities." Yet, according to this study, even men rank relationships at work as their seventh most important work value. And, importantly, "people in lower-level jobs (regardless of gender) are more likely to cite relationships as important."

xlviii   Thurman, R., "Inner Revolution – Life, Liberty, and the Pursuit of Real Happiness," Penguin Putnam (New York) 1998, p. 322.

xlix   *Id.*

l   Niven, David, "The 100 Simple Secrets Of Happy People: What Scientists Have Learned and How You Can Use It," Harper SanFrancisco: 1st edition (May 2, 2000).

li   Happiness is almost always measured "subjectively," that is by simply asking, in one way or another, "How happy are you?" Questions often asked in happiness surveys include:

"In general how happy would you say you are?"

"Taken all together, how happy would you say you are?"

"How happy do you feel as you live now?"

"When somebody would say "this person is very happy" is he right or wrong?"

"Generally speaking, are you a happy person?"

"How happy is your life at this moment?"

See *Veenhoven, Ruut, "Happiness in Nations" RISBO, Erasmus University Rotterdam, 1993, ISBN 90-72597-46-X, Chapter 7.* "Though all these questions use the word 'happiness' as the key-term, they differ subtly in time-perspective ('generally', 'at the moment') and in delineation of the topic ('your life', 'all together'). Such minor differences can of course produce small variations in average scores, which can jeopardize comparisons between nations and through time. The difference in average happiness between nations is mostly not greater than one or two points on a 10 step scale. Differences of one point caused by variation in wording can therefore obscure much of the true differences in happiness across nations.

"Similar variation exists in the phrasing of questions about 'satisfaction-with-life'. Though all these items use the term 'satisfaction', they differ slightly in definition of 'life'. Some refer to 'life-as-a-whole', whereas others are more specific and ask about satisfaction with 'present life' or with 'the life you lead'."

lii   Niven, *supra,* p. 12, citing study by Magen, Birenbaum, and Pery, 1996.

liii   Niven, *supra,* p. 22, citing study by Murray and Peacock, 1996.

liv   Caudron, S., "The Myth Of Job Happiness," Workforce Magazine, February 26, 2001, citing Conference Board.

lv   Lane, Robert, "The Loss Of Happiness In Market Democracies" (Yale University Press: 2000).

lvi   From an article by Davidson, Keay, "Science Tracks the Good Life — It turns out the Bluebird of Happiness roosts in Denmark," San Francisco Chronicle, December 24, 2000, p. A-1.

lvii   Niven, David, *supra,* p. 35, citing study by Hunter and Liao, 1995.

lviii   Niven, David, *supra,* p. 102, citing study by Ferroni and Taffe, 1997

lix   Niven, David, *supra,* p. 54, citing study by Takahashi, Tamura, and Tokora, 1997

lx   Cross, Gary S., "Time and Money — The Making of the Consumer Culture," (Routledge, 1993)

lxi   Lane, Robert, "The Loss Of Happiness In Market Democracies" (Yale University Press: 2000). See Chapter 3, "Why Money Doesn't Buy Happiness For Most Of Us," pp. 59 – 76.

lxii   During the same period worker productivity increased by more than 10 percent. U.S. Bureau Of Labor Statistics, News USDL00-125, Productivity and Costs.

lxiii   Frank, R., Cook, P., "The Winner Take All Society," The Free Press (New York: 1995), p. 86.

lxiv   Pummer, Chris, "Regrowing A Spine," CBSMarketwatch.com, August 14, 2002. "Inflation-adjusted wages have increased marginally in the last quarter century, but the gain has been more than wiped out by contributions to health insurance coverage and 401(k)s — a non-existent expense in the days of fixed pensions. But for a privileged few, prosperity is largely attainable today only for two-income households. Now that the divorce rate runs 50 percent, millions have the added burden of financing two households. 'CEO incomes going through the roof is not news to people doing the real work in America,' said Jonathan Holloway, a labor and social history professor at Yale University. 'But these corporate scandals are lifting the cover a little, and we're seeing how dirty everyone's hands are in this, the politicians as well as corporate executives.'"

lxv   Koretz, G., "Economic Trends: Gen-X Gets Short-changed," BusinessWeek, May 11, 1998, p. 24.

lxvi   The Kaiser Family Foundation/Health Research and Educational Trust, Employer Health Benefits – 2001 Annual Survey.

lxvii   Fraser, J., "White-Collar Sweatshop – The Deterioration of Work and Its Rewards In Corporate America," (New York: W.W. Norton & Co., 2001), p. 60.

lxviii   The Kaiser Family Foundation/Health Research and Educational Trust, Employer Health Benefits – 2001 Annual Survey.

lxix   From American Association of Health Plans, Ind. Choice Model of Health Insurance.

lxx   The Kaiser Family Foundation/Health Research and Educational Trust, Employer Health Benefits – 2001 Annual Survey.

lxxi   National Institute for Health Care Management (Washington, D.C.) as cited in Harper's Magazine, Harper's Index, August, 2001.

lxxii   Gale, Sarah, "How Three Companies Shave Health Care Costs," Workforce Magazine, August, 2001, p. 78-79.

lxxiii   Samuelson, Robert J., "The Pension Time Bomb," Newsweek, 2003.

lxxiv   Kuttner, R., "Pensions: How Much Risk Should Workers Bear?", Business Week, April 16, 2000, p. 23.

lxxv   Fraser, J., "White-Collar Sweatshop – The Deterioration of Work and Its Rewards In Corporate America," (New York: W.W. Norton & Co., 2001), p. 68, f.n. 10.

lxxvi   Trying to make less look like more, many companies continue to spin retirement reality, openly denigrating the defined benefit pension plan as "old-style," and "out-of-date," equivocating it to Social Security and its unconscionably low return, and argument that sounds good, but is untrue. As Robert Frank observed in *Luxury Fever,* "Social security is not a retirement savings program at all, but rather a 'tax-

and-transfer' program. Social Security takes no advantage of compounding interest. Defined benefit plans, when the benefits are defined and the contributions calculated, do take advantage of compounding interest which inures to the benefit of employees covered by these plans."

lxxvii   Barclays Global Investors, "Why Defined Contribution Plans Underperform Defined Benefit Plans, and How To Fix Them," Investment Insights, April, 2000. cited by Scott Burns, "401(k) May Yield Smaller Next Egg Than Pension," Dallas Morning News, April 25, 2001, p. 1D.

lxxviii   *Id.* at p. 1D, 6D.

lxxix   Federal Reserve, Survey of Consumer Finances.

lxxx   Cobb (CNBC), Jerry, "Companies Start To Trim 401(k) Contributions" MSNBC News, October 2, 2001.

lxxxi   Braham, "Company Stock Could Sink Your Ship," BusinessWeek, July 30, 2001, p. 86.

lxxxii   Few employers offer education to employees on investing their assets, however many employee assistance programs report an increase incidence of requests for assistance on financial matters. "Forty percent of all work-life calls (not related to mental health) made by workers were related to financial help, up from 26 percent a year earlier, according to ComPsych, a Chicago-based employee assistance provider covering about 25 million people worldwide." See Coombes, Andrea, "Dialing For Help With Dollars," CBSMarketWatch.com, February 18, 2004.

lxxxiii   Andrews, M., and McGregor, J., "The Best and Worst 401(k)'s," SmartMoney Magazine, October 2000, p. 134, finding that Lowe's, the home improvement chain, offered a 12-fund selection that underperformed funds of a similar type. Cited at the bottom of the heap is Lucent which does not provide certain key investment options such as an S&P 500 Index Fund or a small-cap fund. Other laggards were Johnson & Johnson, which permits employees to change investments only once every three months, and HCA, which makes a maximum contribution of $1,000 per year to an employee's account, and five companies – PepsiCo, AMR, Caterpillar, Xerox, and TIAA-CREF that didn't (at the time of the article) contribute anything to their employees' 401(k) accounts. Companies like Texaco and Eastman Kodak, to the contrary, were cited for "best plans" based on the ability to enroll immediately, generous corporate matches, and well-performing funds.

lxxxiv   Loeb, Marshall, "Childcare expenses make work unprofitable for many," CBS.MarketWatch.com, Aug 8, 2003. "Over the last two decades, the number of stay-at-home fathers raising children has gone up 70 percent, according to census data. While societal norms are changing, the cost of child care can influence a parent's decision to stay at home. Many couples think that when they have children, the family budget won't allow either parent to stop working. In fact, when the costs of working are itemized, it may make more financial sense to stay at home. With the going rate for live-out nannies between $8 and $15 an hour, it can be a challenge to just break even. Live-in nannies are typically paid $400 and $800 to week, according to Lora Brawley, owner of the nanny agency, Brawley & Associates in Baltimore. Commuting expenses and the cost of work clothes can make working appear even less profitable. Other financial obligations inherent in hiring a nanny include paying the employer's portion of Social Security and Medicare. Annual costs of sending a child to a day care center run from about $4,000 to $10,000 a year."

lxxxv   See Kuttner, R., "Pensions: How Much Risk Should Workers Bear?," BusinessWeek, April 26, 2001, p. 23.

lxxxvi   IBM and Citigroup both outsource heavily, having invested in India-based offshore outsourcing contractors, with an intent to sell offshoring services to other companies, to include low cost software development, as well as customer relations and human-resources functions. Tarsala, Mike, "Buying Into Outsourcing," CBS.Marketwatch.com, April 16, 2004. Interestingly, the offshoring of American jobs goes on without the objection, and indeed with the imprimatur of the Bush Administration, the President seemingly endorsing the concept after signing a report in early 2004 that touted overseas outsourcing despite more than 8 million Americans being out of work and even in light of a study showing that up to 14 million American jobs could be lost to outsourcing in the coming years unless the process is slowed. *See* "Outsourcing Hits Close to Home for Workers in Northwest Ohio," Miami Herald, March 14, 2004.

lxxxvii   U.S. Census Bureau, Statistical Abstract Of The United States: 2000, No. 689. Productivity and Related Measures: 1980 to 1999.

lxxxviii   Report: "The State of Working America," Economic Policy Institute, 2002.

lxxxix   Cook, Philip, and Frank, Robert, "The Winner-Take-All Society: Why the Few at the Top Get So Much More Than the Rest of Us," Penguin USA (September 1996), p. 38.

xc   U.S. Census Bureau, Statistical Abstract Of The United States, 2000, Table 831, p. 525.

xci   Tasini, Jonathan, "The Wal-Mart Myth," Tompaine.com, April 13, 2004.

xcii   "A study completed by the American Management Association concluded that only about half the companies that undertake restructuring activities, including employee downsizings, experience any long-term improvement in earnings following the restructuring. Still, corporate executives have commonly received large compensation increases almost immediately following cost-cutting announcements." Responsible Wealth, The Shareholder Resolution Campaign 2000-2001.

xciii   The Conference Board, "Compensation Of Outside Directors and CEO's," Press Release November 27, 2000. "Companies are emphasizing the stock component of top executive compensation . . . in the belief that increase in share value is a primary indicator of company performance. In particular, they are making significant grants of stock options." The value of CEO option grants in 1999 ranged from 89 percent of base salary in stock insurance companies to 245 percent in computer services. With the exception of insurance, all industry sectors reported grants with values greater than 100 percent of salary. CEO bonuses for 1999 were greatest in transportation and computer services. Transportation CEOs received 119 percent of salary; in computer services they received 110 percent."

xciv   According to Bloomberg, in 2003 executive pay in 70 of the top 100 companies rose to an average of $14.1 million. That is 384 years of the average employee's pay of $36,764, and 525 years of earnings of Joe Lunchbucket, production worker, who averages $26,902. Total CEO pay at these 70 companies rose 7.5 percent in 2003, while employee pay inched up a mere 1.5% as the U.S. economy lost 410,000 jobs.

xcv   Armour, Stephanie, "Workers asked to train foreign replacements," USA Today, April 6, 2004. "In the next 15 years, American employers will move about 3.3 million white-collar jobs and $136 billion in wages abroad, according to Forrester Research. That's up from $4 billion in wages in 2000."

xcvi   Harper's Index, Harper's Magazine, May, 2000, pp. 13, 86.

xcvii   Walsh, Mary, "Factory Workers Fight The Squeeze On Health Benefits," New York Times, October 25, 2000, p. 2, 10.

xcviii   Incentive Magazine cited by Haskell, Jack, "Dimension Of Retention," Journal Of Workplace Management, 2000.

xcix   "At Southwest, Storied Culture Is Showing Signs Of Strain," The Wall Street Journal, Friday, July 11, 2003, pp. A1, A6.

c   Shull, Brenda Dean, "Good Management Matters – Study Unveil People Leave Managers, Not Companies," Smartpros, July 24, 2000.

ci   Marcus Buckingham and Curt Coffman, "First, Break All The Rules," Simon & Schuster, 1999.

cii   Studies cited by Kevin Dobbs, "Knowing How To Keep Your Best And Brightest," Workforce Magazine, April 2001, pp. 57-60.

ciii   From interview with Marcus Buckingham in Fast Company magazine, November, 2000.

civ   Burt, R. S., Strangers, Friends, and Happiness, GSS Technical Report No. 72, Chicago: National Opinion Research Center, University of Chicago, 1986.

cv   After hours peaked at 60 hours a week in 1890, hours of work fell to 40 by 1950 where it held steady until 1973. By 1988, the American worker averaged forty-seven hours a week, during a period when leisure time shrank 37 per cent. Zelinski, E., "The Joy Of Not Working," (Berkeley, CA.: Ten Speed Press) 1997, pp. 65, 127, 137. And, even when managers take vacation today, they don't take much and they are rarely untethered from their offices. "According to a recent 2004 survey by the American Management Association, only 32 percent of managers surveyed said they'd take 6 to 10 days off consecutively this summer. More than half (58 percent) said they wouldn't take off more than 5 days consecutively. Twenty-four percent of all managers surveyed said they contact the office daily when they're on vacation. Another 28 percent said they check in every two to three days." Sadahi, Jeanne, "Why Don't You Take A 2-Week Vacation," CNN Money, June 7, 2004.

cvii   DeGraff, John, "Workweek Woes," New York Times, April 13, 2003. "What happened? In effect, the United States as a society took all of its increases in labor productivity in the form of money and stuff instead of time. Of course, we didn't all get the money; the very poor earn even less in real terms than they did then, and the largest share of the increase went to the richest Americans."

cviii   Quoted by Caudron, Shari, Workforce Magazine, April, 2001, "The Myth Of Job Happiness," p. 36.

cix   A poem sent to us by one first-line manager describes his feelings about upper management. It is not happenstance that we receive so many diatribes along these lines from managers who recognize the inherent conflicts between and among upper management, middle management, and employees.

"It is funny I think
To watch how THEY walk around all day
Holding their crotches like their dicks were Excalibur.
Hoping upon hope we will bow down before their might and

grandeur!
Pitiful souls these high gods on thrones of dog shit
"Strive to be me" tattooed on their hairy asses in
neon letters like a Vegas show sign.
How they scurry about when the real corporate gods
come holding their dicks of gold in hand.
CHOP, CHOP, CHOP the sound of heads rolling down the
endless stacks of bricks.
Blood flows crimson in the Texas sun, all around my feet!
"We need new gods," the golden one
screams to the others in a crackled voice!
All the while I, in the background, get new material
to make me laugh while I shit in the morning".

cx   See, Thoms, Dose, & Scott, "Relationships between Accountability, Job Satisfaction and Trust," Academy of Management, Toronto, October, 2000.

cxi   R. S. Wurman, "Information Anxiety," Doubleday: 1989.

cxii   See, Information/Work Overload Annotated Webliography, www.softpanorama.org/social/overload.shtml.

cxiii   Waddington, P. "Dying for information: an investigation of information overload in the UK and world-wid,". Reuters Business Information. 1996

cxiv   Jeremy Rifkin, "The Age Of Access," Tarcher/Putnam, 2000, p. 84, citing James Brian Quinn, "Intelligent Enterprise: A Knowledge and Service Based Paradigm For Industry" (New York: The Free Press, 1992), p. 30.

cxv   From, "Mental Health: A Report Of The Surgeon General." ww.surgeongeneral.gov/library/mentalhealth/chater4/sec1_1.html.

cxvi   *Id.,* "Mental Health: A Report Of the Surgeon General," Chapter 4 – Adults and Mental Health, citing Kim & Jacobs, 1995.)

cxvii   Cicely Saunders, the pioneer of the hospice movement in Britain, wrote: "I once asked a man who knew he was dying what he needed above all in those who were caring for him. He said, 'For someone to look as if they are trying to understand me.' Indeed, it is impossible to understand fully another person, but I never forgot that he did not ask for success but only that someone should care enough to try."

cxviii Whatever the significance, birthday observances date back to pagan cultures when birthdays were occasions celebrated with family and friends who surrounded the person of honor with laughter and joy in order to protect them from evil spirits. From that day to this, birthdays have retained significance in our lives and we anticipate those who care for us to mark the event by acknowledging our birthdays.

cxix   *Supra,* from "Mental Health: A Report Of The Surgeon General," Chapter 4 – Adults and Mental Health, citing Holmes and Rahe, 1967; Lazarus & Folkman, 1984; Kreiger et al., 1993.

cxx   *Id.*

cxxi   *Id.,* from "Mental Health: A Report Of the Surgeon General," Chapter 4 – Adults and Mental Health, citing Brown & Harris, 1989.

cxxi   "Census Finds Living Together Without Marriage On The Rise," The Ft. Worth Star iTelegram, May 20, 2001, p. 6A.

cxxiii While "living wage" legislation has been passed in a relative handful of communities that compels employers to pay above the poverty line, employers in low-paying industries have wailed and predicted economic Armageddon if they are compelled to pay their employees enough to provide basic food, shelter, and clothing for their families, and to this date industry has been successful in the political battle over the minimum wage which, while up 6.7% between 1989 and 1998, is only playing catch up, having fallen 16.1% between 1979 and 1989 on an inflation-adjusted basis. U.S. Census Bureau, Current Population Reports, 1998, p. 50-201.

cxxiv "What Exactly Is A 'Living Wage'?", BusinessWeek, May 28, 2001, p. 78.

cxxv The wide and intense range of feelings after being victimized by violence can lead to emotional outbursts at any time, including work time, and the effects of crime may last for years. Nightmares, insomnia, periods of uncontrolled sobbing, occasional hysterical laughter, nausea, headaches, fatigue or a feeling of going insane are not uncommon in serious cases. Family relationships may suffer as individuals react differently to the same trauma, leading to mental, physical, and financial stress, resulting in discord, divorce, alcohol abuse, and a variety of other problems. Moving, quitting work, becoming pregnant, and divorcing are common responses and these changes add more stress to an already stressful existence.

cxxvi See "A Handbook For Victims Of Crime in Alaska,", September, 2001, published by Alaska Judicial Council, http://www.ajc.state.ak.us/Reports/victmanframe.htm

cxxvii "Domestic violence costs companies an estimated $5 million annually as violence at home spills over into the workplace for nearly 100 percent of employed victims. The crime of domestic violence not only causes decreased productivity, errors and absenteeism, it also affects other employees with danger increasing the level of fear and distraction. Increased health costs, turnover and employee time spent away from production to cope with problems increase due to domestic violence." Purcell, Regina, *The Record-Courier,* April 21, 2004.

xxiv Weil, Simone, "The Mystery of the Factory," Factory Journal, (1934–35; reprinted in La Condition Ouvrière, 1951).

cxxix Hendricks, G., Ludeman, K., "The Corporate Mystic," Bantam Books: New York, 1996, p. 143.

cxxx "Power tends to corrupt, and absolute power corrupts absolutely. Great men are almost always bad men." Lord Acton (1834–1902), English historian. Letter, 3 April 1887, to Bishop Mandell Creighton (published in *The Life and Letters of Mandell Creighton,* 1904). William Pitt the Elder had previously said something to the same effect, in a speech to the House of Lords, 9 Jan. 1770: "Unlimited power is apt to corrupt the minds of those who possess it."

cxxxi "If we had no faults of our own, we should not take so much pleasure in noticing those in others." François, Duc de La Rochefoucauld, *Sentences et Maximes Morales,* no. 31 (1678).

cxxxii Halkias, Maria, "Former Wal-Mart Exec, Daughter Push for Workplace Ethics," Dallas Morning News, May 22, 2001, p. 2D.

cxxxiii Letter, 1 Jan. 1910, to Pound's mother. Quoted in: Humphrey Carpenter, *A Serious Character,* pt. 5, ch. 6 (1988).

cxxxiv Carpenter, Liz, "The Last Word - A Treasury of Women's Quotes," 1992.

cxxxv Rifkin, Jeremy "The Age Of Access, " (New York: Tarcher/Putnam 2000), p. 205.

cxxxvi Williams, Jennifer, "The Pleasures Of Staying In Touch," Hearst Books, 1998, pp. 12-13.

cxxxvii "At Southwest, Storied Culture Is Showing Signs Of Strain," The Wall Street Journal, Friday, July 11, 2003, pp. A1, A6.

cxxxviii From interview in *Writers at Work* (First Series, ed. by Malcolm Cowley, 1958).

cxxxix Conference Board, "HR Executive Review: Employee Recognition Programs," as reported in news release dated January 24, 2000.

cxl From letter of December 7, 1906 to Joyce's brother, published in *Letters of James Joyce,* vol. 2, 1966.

cxli Handy, Charles, *supra,* The Gods Of Management, p. 227.

cxlii Lykken, D., "Happiness," St. Martin's Press (1999), p. 181.

cxliii Miller, Henry, "The Books in My Life," ch. 12 (1951).

cxliv Coolidge, Calvin, Speech, January 17, 1925, to the Society of American Newspaper Editors.

cxlv Tawney, R.H., as quoted by Schumacher, E.F. in "Small Is Beautiful," Harper Row (1973), p. 279.

cxlvi Marin Independent Journal, "Despite gains, women still earn less than men," Associated Press Report of June 4, 2004. According to the most recent census report, few jobs offer salary parity. Indeed, "the median income for a woman working full-time, year-round was about $28,000, compared with $38,000 for a man. That means a woman earned fewer than 74 cents for every dollar earned by a man." Also see Kirchoff, Sue, "Minorities haven't felt economic growth," USA Today, June 16, 2004. "Minorities lag behind whites in employment and earnings more than two years after the 2001 recession officially ended. African-Americans in particular have taken a big hit: suffering higher and longer unemployment than whites and dropping out of the labor force more rapidly."

cxlvii Hoffer, Eric, "The Passionate State of Mind," aph. 123 (1955).

Printed in the United States
31540LVS00001BA/316-366

9 781589 612587